# Thomas Jefferson
## Man with a Vision

# Thomas Jefferson

## Man with a Vision

by Ruth Crisman

SCHOLASTIC INC.
New York Toronto London Auckland Sydney

**Picture Credits**

Cover: Courtesy of the Independence National Historical Park Collection.

Interiors: Frontispiece and pages 39, 49, 60, 76, 78, and 95, Library of Congress. Pages 7, 48, 51, and 93, New York Public Library. Page 9, Tuckahoe Plantation. Page 22, North Wind Picture Archives. Pages 25, 105, 132, 136, and 140, Thomas Jefferson Memorial Foundation, Inc. Page 28, Colonial Williamsburg Foundation. Page 31, United Press International. Pages 47 and 91, Brown Brothers. Pages 53 and 112, New York Historical Society. Page 64, Maryland Historical Society. Page 66, Yale University Art Gallery. Page 84, National Gallery of Art. Pages 106 and 134, University of Virginia Library. Page 110, Museum of Fine Arts, Boston. Page 117, National Portrait Gallery. Page 128, Harvard College Library. Page 139, West Point Museum Collection.

ISBN 0-590-44553-7

Copyright © 1992 by Ruth Crisman. All rights reserved. Published by Scholastic Inc.

12 11 10 9 8 7 6 5 4 3 2 1          2 3 4 5 6 7/9

Printed in the U.S.A.          40

First Scholastic printing, December 1992

To Meredith Brucker

# Contents

# Prologue:
# Thomas Jefferson

His giant image is carved on the granite walls of Mount Rushmore in South Dakota. On every nickel, a small portrait of Jefferson appears on one side of the coin, and his home, Monticello, on the other. His inspiring, patriotic words are enshrined on the walls of the Jefferson Memorial Monument in Washington, D.C. The American people honor Thomas Jefferson, the third president, for dedicated service to his country.

When English colonists revolted against British rule, the Second Continental Congress asked Jefferson to draft the Declaration of Independence. He is called "America's architect" for his special part in shaping the nation.

Jefferson was one of America's first great architects in many ways. As well as other structures, Jefferson designed and built his remarkable home and plantation, Monticello, over a period of forty years. He is reported to have said: "Architecture is my delight, and putting up and pulling down one of my favorite amusements." Each year, thousands of travelers visit his Monticello estate where Jefferson spent his happiest years.

As a statesman, Thomas Jefferson served his country as governor of Virginia, minister to France, secretary of state, vice president, and president of the United States. One of his most important executive decisions was the Louisiana Purchase, the acquisition from France of the biggest piece of real estate in America.

Jefferson was an unusually gifted man of many interests and talents. This lean, muscular, 6'2" lawyer and leader found time for such occupations as gardening, geography, architecture, astronomy, mechanics, and music. During his lifetime of eighty-three years, he read thousands of books and wrote thousands of letters to colonists, statesmen, family, and friends.

Jefferson spoke through his pen, and his letters and records tell us what he cared about most. With deep faith and confidence, he believed the people should run their own government, and his document of freedom has lasted through the ages.

# 1
## *The Boy Jefferson*
## *1743–1757*

**T**homas Jefferson was born at Shadwell, in the backcountry of Virginia, on April 13, 1743. His father, Peter Jefferson, had surveyed and cleared the land, built a wooden farmhouse, and brought his family to live there. Peter named the house Shadwell after the parish in London where his wife, Jane Randolph, had been christened.

At that time, Peter Jefferson owned more than a thousand acres of farmland and forest tended by slaves. Shadwell was located between the foothills of the Blue Ridge Mountains, less than thirty miles away, and the western edge of the Tidewater, land near the sea, another eighty or so miles farther. The house looked southward toward the Rivanna River, which was the north branch of the James River.

In 1737 Peter Jefferson had been the third or

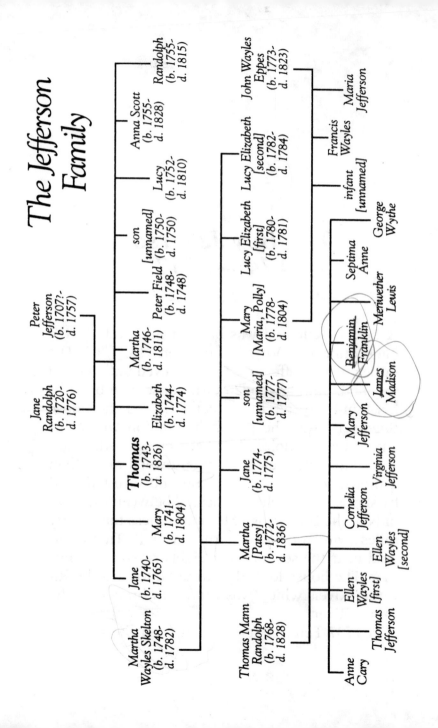

# The Jefferson Family

fourth settler in that part of Goochland County, now called Albemarle County. Of Welsh descent from a pioneer family in Virginia, he was self-educated as a surveyor, mapmaker, and planter. He belonged to the yeomanry, a class of English freeholders, or property holders, who ranked below the gentry.

Peter Jefferson was close friends with William Randolph, a young Virginian whose immense property adjoined his to the east. William had introduced Peter to his cousin, Jane Randolph. Her father, Isham Randolph, a sea captain, owned thousands of acres on the James River. The Randolphs traced their heritage back to England and Scotland, and they were considered one of the leading families in Virginia, part of the aristocratic class, or gentry.

Isham's daughter Jane had been born in England, and Peter was a man of the backcountry. But Isham believed that Peter was a responsible person and trusted him. When Peter became sheriff, Isham Randolph and his young nephew William Randolph had signed Peter's bond of 1000 pounds sterling. This bond affirmed that Jefferson was an honest man and would perform his duties faithfully. Besides keeping order, the sheriff collected the king's revenue from the county. If Peter Jefferson absconded with the tax receipts, the signers were liable for the bond money.

Jane was nineteen and Peter thirty-two years old when they married. The Randolphs would one day provide an influential family connection for Peter's unborn son, Thomas.

Although little is written about Jane Randolph Jefferson, it is known that she was a modest, refined Virginia lady. She loved to garden, and wrote many letters to her family about her married life on the remote plantation. Jane and Peter already had two daughters when they moved to Shadwell, but the birth of their first son, Thomas, was greatly welcomed. According to English custom, the first son would receive his father's inheritance.

Young Tom possessed good health, and his father's strength and agility. Under Peter Jefferson's influence, Tom learned to be diligent in his studies, to say his prayers, and to read the Bible. As he was growing up, Tom loved horses, and his father taught him to ride well. Thomas Jefferson was regarded as one of the finest horsemen of his day.

The forest area of Goochland County was wild and unsettled, a place where Tom could hear a wolf call for miles. He especially enjoyed climbing through the forest to his lookout point on "little mountain." From there he could see everywhere, all the mountains and valleys, his father's house, and the plantation below. Tom dreamed that someday he would build a house on his mountaintop and, years later, he would make the dream come true.

When Peter Jefferson was home, Tom went hunting with his father for deer and wild turkey. The children played in the open countryside and

*An eighteenth-century illustration depicting tobacco farming, Virginia's leading industry.*

often Tom paddled a canoe or fished in the Rivanna River nearby.

Below the Rivanna on the James River, English ships arrived loaded with articles for the colonists in the Tidewater area. The wooden vessels brought such items as furniture, letters, barrels of china, and books, then returned to England with tobacco from the plantations. In 1743, the valuable crop of tobacco played a major role in the Virginia economy. Landowners prospered by farming the rich land with slave labor.

Virginia was the largest of the thirteen colonies in the New World, stretching west through forests to the Allegheny Mountains, a western part of the Appalachians. The main road to Williamsburg, the capital city, was a dirt highway that ran east and west near the Jefferson plantation. Shadwell was a stopping-off place for pioneers, soldiers, and Indians on their way to and from the colonial capital, and the Jeffersons welcomed them. Peter Jefferson invited Chief Outassette of the Cherokee tribe for dinner many times.

Like his father, young Tom made friends and enjoyed playing with the young Indian braves. Chief Outassette gave him a present of a beautifully carved paddle for his canoe, which Tom treasured for many years.

The ride east to the Tidewater usually took Peter Jefferson two days. The journey's length depended on the weather, the number of stops, the horses, and the condition of roads and rivers. Besides Peter Jefferson's work in the Tidewater, he went to visit his friend William Randolph at his Tuckahoe plantation. Randolph's large estate was located just west of Richmond on a bluff overlooking the James River valley. Randolph made a request in his will that when he died, his "dear and loving friend," Peter Jefferson, would move down to Tuckahoe with his children.

Peter promised to take care of Randolph's family and to see to their education, especially that of his son, Thomas Mann Randolph. There were no schools on the frontier, for people lived too far from each other and children were needed to help at home on the smaller farms. Only the gentry could afford to send their children to a private school or have them tutored. Usually the teachers were clergymen, and the pupils were sons of landowners.

After William Randolph died at the early age of thirty-three (there is no record why), Peter Jefferson kept his promise and moved his own family to Tuckahoe. Many years later, Thomas Jefferson said that he remembered the time when he was two years old and a slave held him on a pillow as they rode by horseback to the plantation.

In his will, William Randolph had provided that the children were to have their own private school. There were three young Randolphs — Thomas Mann, Judith, and Mary — along with four young Jeffersons now. The two Toms quickly became friends.

For their education, Peter Jefferson hired a pri-

*Thomas Jefferson's schoolhouse on Tuckahoe Plantation.*

vate tutor and the children began their studies in one of the outbuildings behind the mansion house. At age five, Tom Jefferson began to read, write, and do arithmetic problems with his cousins. The Jeffersons' little schoolhouse still stands at Tuckahoe, which continues to operate today as a working plantation after 275 years.

Everything at Tuckahoe was on a much grander scale than at Shadwell. Many more barrels (called "hogsheads") were shipped to England from Tuckahoe than from the Jefferson estate. Peter Jefferson directed the duties of several overseers who reported the amount of tobacco produced on the farm to him.

The plantation was Tom's first introduction to the hierarchy of whites and blacks in the South at that time. What was he thinking as he watched the slaves at work? Men, women, and children planted the fields, cured the tobacco, and served as cooks, tailors, coachmen, and carpenters. And none had the freedom to leave if they didn't like the working conditions.

For all his ideals of "justice for all," Thomas Jefferson was a slaveholder. In their years of service to him on the plantation, his slaves learned trades and were treated better than most at that time. However, during his lifetime, Thomas Jefferson never freed his slaves and, at his death, freed only a few.

While the families stayed at the Randolph estate, Peter Jefferson surveyed and mapped several areas of Virginia. In 1749, Peter Jefferson and Joshua

10

Fry, a mathematics professor, surveyed the dividing point between Virginia and North Carolina for ninety miles, crossing small streams and several ranges of mountains.

Stories about this trip became a tradition, often repeated to children and grandchildren. Tom probably heard the men talking about their hardships: riding horseback, climbing the narrow jutted peaks of the Blue Ridge Mountains, encountering dangerous wild beasts by day, and sleeping in the trees at night.

Sometimes his father took Tom with him on short trips. As Peter made his calculations and drew maps of the area, Tom learned the art of surveying, what instruments were used, how lines were measured. Peter Jefferson and Joshua Fry were considered especially qualified surveyors by the governor. Their maps contributed to the geographical knowledge of Virginia and were distributed in England.

Many years later, in his *Notes on Virginia*, Thomas Jefferson referred the reader to the Fry-Jefferson map, writing, "the mountains are not solitary and scattered confusedly over the face of the country, but are disposed in ridges one behind another."

In 1752, after seven busy years at Tuckahoe, Peter Jefferson took his family back to Shadwell. His wife Jane kept busy with domestic crafts, household duties, and caring for their children. Tom was nine now and had two older sisters, Jane and Mary, as well as four younger sisters, Elizabeth, Martha, Lucy, and Anna Scott. His only brother, Randolph, was born in 1755. When they were older, Tom became more like a father to Randolph, who was apparently retarded.

Jane Jefferson had lost two of her ten children in childbirth while the family lived at Tuckahoe. In colonial days, many children died of childhood diseases, such as malaria, before the doctor could reach them. The frontier woman lived with the ever-present fear for her health and the health of her family. Pregnancy posed a problem for women, isolated in their homes with no doctor or midwife.

To continue Tom's education, Peter Jefferson sent him to Latin school in Northam. He lived there for five years, returning home only for vacations. Scottish clergyman William Douglas taught him the classical languages, Greek and Latin, and also some French. Tom learned etiquette, as well as how to play the violin and how to dance.

Even at a young age, Tom was always curious about the local trees and plants both large and small, and knew the names of most of those grown in central Virginia. From this early interest, he would later design his beautiful gardens at Monticello.

In 1757, when Tom was fourteen, his father died at the age of fifty. Peter Jefferson did not follow tradition and leave his estate to his eldest son. He divided it between Tom and Randolph. The land included the 867-foot-high "little mountain," where Tom had played as a child.

In his will, Peter left some 7500 acres in four or five different parcels of land, twenty-one horses, a number of hogs and cows, and fifty-three slaves. To his wife, he left the house and lands at Shadwell, one-sixth of the household goods and slaves, two workhorses, and one-third of the livestock on the plantation.

Each of the six daughters inherited a slave as a personal servant and "200 pounds sterling," to be paid as a dowry when each one reached twenty-two years of age.

Thomas and his younger brother, Randolph, inherited the remaining slaves. The livestock was to be sold to pay for the boys' education. In his will, Peter Jefferson asked that his sons be given a classical education, the education that Peter wished he had received. Among the forty or more books he left was a well-worn edition of Shakespeare.

Tom also inherited his father's leadership ability. Peter Jefferson had served his community as a surveyor, mapmaker, magistrate, sheriff, colonel of the militia, and member of the colonial House of Burgesses from the county of Albemarle.

Twenty years later, Thomas Jefferson would follow his father's example, beginning his career by representing his neighbors in the Virginia legislature at Williamsburg.

As a teenager, young Tom felt the loss of his father intensely. This is what he wrote later in life: "When I realized that at fourteen years of age the whole care and direction of myself was thrown on myself entirely . . . and recollect the various sorts of bad company with which I associated from time to time . . . I am astonished that I did not turn off with some of them."

# 2
# Education for a Gentleman
# 1757–1767

Although he would not inherit his father's estate until he was twenty-one years old, Thomas Jefferson was now considered the head of the family. At fourteen, the teenager was strong and tall with a freckled face, reddish hair, and large hands and feet. A little awkward, he was slow to speak and expressed himself best on paper.

After his father's death, his guardians sent him to study with the Reverend James Maury, one of the most scholarly clergymen in the colony. Maury lived on a plantation about fourteen miles from Shadwell and, besides doing church work, helped support his family by instructing planters' sons. Tom boarded at Maury's home and attended class in a small log house on the plantation for a period of two years.

Young Jefferson liked his new teacher and

thought him more accomplished in languages than his previous teacher, clergyman Douglas. Jefferson had a natural gift for learning different tongues, and after Maury's training in the classical languages, he was able to read Greek and Roman authors in the original for the rest of his life.

Besides Latin and Greek, clergyman Maury taught his class of five students history, geography, mathematics, and farming. But there was also time each day for the boys to ride horses or hike with friends beneath the Southwest Mountains.

Sometimes other boys, including Tom's close friend, Dabney Carr, went home with Tom on weekends. In the summer they swam in the river and rode their horses in the woods. Tom loved to race horses, but his slow pony could never beat Dabney's swift one.

However, one day Tom bet his pony could beat Dabney's in a race, and set the date for February 30. Dabney was sure that he would win, and waited for the day to arrive. Suddenly he realized he had been tricked! There were only twenty-eight days in February, and he forfeited the race.

Growing up together, Dabney and Tom developed a lasting friendship. Sometimes the two boys would climb Tom's favorite mountain, sit under an oak tree, and talk or study their books. Other times they just looked out at the beautiful countryside. One day they made a pledge to each other that whoever died first would be buried under their oak tree on "little mountain."

\* \* \*

Jefferson began to wonder if he should be doing more with his life. In January of 1760 he visited his mother's cousin, Peter Randolph, who was also one of his guardians. Encouraged by Randolph to go to college, he wrote his business manager, John Harvie, requesting the money. Harvie consented and decided that Tom should begin studies at William and Mary College.

Jefferson packed his saddlebags full of books and music, and asked his slave Jupiter, who rode behind him, to carry his fiddle. After saying goodbye to his family, he set off by horseback across country the 120 miles or so to Williamsburg. The college he would attend was named for the former

*An early illustration of the College of William and Mary, which Jefferson attended.*

reigning King William and Queen Mary, who had chartered it under the auspices of the Church of England. Founded in 1693, it was the second oldest college in the English colonies, after Harvard University.

Williamsburg was a whole new world for this seventeen-year-old. At first Jefferson followed the social activities of the other students who liked to play cards, race their horses, go fox hunting, or spend money on fine clothes. There were young ladies, parties, theater, and musicales. Jefferson was more outgoing now, and popular.

At the end of the first summer, Jefferson went home for a short vacation. Getting ready to go back to Williamsburg, he was happy to hear that Dabney Carr would return with him. As the friends talked about school, Jefferson suddenly realized that he had wasted his time and tuition money amusing himself. He resolved to do better and study his subjects seriously.

He wrote, "I had the good fortune to become acquainted very early with some characters of very high standing, and to feel the incessant wish that I could ever become what they were. Under temptation and difficulties, I would ask myself what would Dr. Small, Mr. Wythe, Peyton Randolph [Jefferson's cousin] do in this situation?"

At William and Mary, Jefferson took classes from Professor William Small of Scotland, who taught most of the curriculum, including science, mathematics, languages, and philosophy. Small spent extra time with his enthusiastic student, opening his mind to the nature of the universe. When Jefferson was much older, he wrote that Professor Small "probably fixed the destinies of my life." Small introduced Jefferson to the work of Isaac Newton, the English mathematician and astronomer; to the work of Francis Bacon, English philosopher and statesman; and to the writings of John Locke, another English philosopher. Small taught Thomas about a new pattern of thought called the "Enlightenment," which was then current in Europe.

Locke had written about this revolutionary philosophy: "Since reason is the only sure guide that God has given to man, reason is the only foundation of a just government. . . . Since governments exist for men, not men for governments, all governments derive their just powers from the consent of the governed."

Under Small's tutoring, mathematics became Jefferson's favorite subject, and he began to carry a box of instruments, a book of logarithms, and a ruler in his pocket when he traveled. Both teacher and friend to Jefferson, Small introduced him to a select group of influential people, one of them, George Wythe, acting attorney general for Virginia. Wythe took Jefferson to the Governor's Palace to meet Francis Fauquier, the governor of Virginia from England.

During his visits, Governor Fauquier, Jefferson, Small, and Wythe had many discussions about art, the theater, or problems of taxation. Listening to Governor Fauquier, Jefferson learned about England and the political world outside of Virginia.

Governor Fauquier and Jefferson shared a love of music, and Fauquier invited Jefferson to play with him in amateur chamber music concerts held weekly in the parlor at the Palace. Sometimes Jefferson's cousin John Randolph played first violin and Jefferson second. John Page, a close friend from William and Mary, also joined the group occasionally.

Often Jefferson spent weekends with John Page at his family home, practicing the violin. John came from a rich and influential family that lived at Rosewell in Gloucester County. John was distantly related to William Randolph, the friend of Jefferson's father. The young men were almost like brothers and their friendship lasted fifty years.

When Jefferson was in Williamsburg, he frequently visited the printing office, where he purchased books and music. The *Virginia Gazette* newspaper was printed there once a week and contained news of England and the colony. It also advertised the sale of horses and of slaves from Africa, as well as notices of runaway slaves.

The many small shops along Duke of Gloucester Street carried a variety of goods. In John Greenhow's store, Jefferson could purchase "commonplace" books, ordinary blank notebooks for school, as well as imported items from England.

An advertising flyer on the store counter listed the items: "Just Imported from LONDON, And to be sold by John Greenhow, at his Store near the

Church in Williamsburg for ready money only, . . . Stuffs of different Kinds for womens gowns, Ready made shirts, Fine Night Caps, Blankets of all sorts and sizes, Fine mens stockings, Feathers for Ladies Hats, Lace of all Kinds, Blank Books unruled of all sizes, Sealing Wax, Inkstands, Pencils, Playing Cards, Licorice, Fine Chocolate, Candlesticks, Tinware . . . Pewter plates . . . All sorts of cast iron."

A rivalry existed between the college students, who were sons of gentlemen with an income, and the boys working in town or learning their fathers' trades. Many of the college students looked down their noses at the apprentices, while many apprentices scorned the bookish boys who wore gowns and attended college.

The hard feelings resulted in a number of fights. On one occasion, tempers were so hot that some college boys swaggered forth carrying sticks and rocks, ready to attack the apprentices in town. There was almost a riot, until Attorney General Peyton Randolph intervened, preventing the violence from getting out of hand.

The boys living at the college had a busy schedule. Up early, they went to chapel services first, then classes all day, with an hour or so free after dinner. Most ate at the hall, seated in their proper order at tables: masters at the head table, divinity students together, then scholars, philosophy students, grammar students, and servitors working their way through college. Sometimes a fencing master or dancing master came in to give lessons.

21

*A minuet being performed at an eighteenth-century gathering.*

Jefferson was probably taught minuets, reels, and country dances.

If the students went to town after dinner, they would hear the Wren Building bell ring at the college to remind them when to return. At nine o'clock each evening the students were required to be present and accounted for, in their nightshirts and ready for bed.

Professor Small had been Jefferson's teacher, advisor, and friend for two years when he decided to return to his home in England. Jefferson felt sorry to see him go and afterward felt that college had nothing more to offer him.

Small had encouraged Jefferson to study law. So in 1762, Jefferson began his legal studies under attorney George Wythe at his home. Some of his subjects included history, political science, philosophy, French, Latin, mathematics, and English law. As he studied with George Wythe, he kept two commonplace books: one contained his ideas on law and government, and the other, literary extracts from Greek, Latin, and English classics.

True to his father's influence, Thomas had learned to be diligent in his studies. His day began at five o'clock in the morning, and he studied past midnight. When he had free time Jefferson played his fiddle, went swimming, and attended dances.

That Christmas, Jefferson stayed at the home of a wealthy friend, and he brought along his fiddle and rolls of minuet music to entertain the guests. The great house was in a state of decay, and its walls a home for rats. In one of his letters to friend John Page, Jefferson complained, "Do you think the cursed rats . . . did not eat up my pocketbook, which was in my pocket, within a foot of my head? And not contented with plenty for the present, they carried away my jemmy-worked [skillfully made] silk garters, and a half a dozen new minuets. . . ."

Perhaps worst of all, it had rained that night and, when he awoke, Jefferson's watch was floating in water that had leaked in from the roof. The watch contained a profile, cut from black paper, of a girl he admired, Rebecca Burwell. Much to his dismay, the soaked picture fell apart when he tried to retrieve it. Jefferson had courted Rebecca and tried to ask her to marry him — but he had been unable to get the words out of his mouth.

On April 13, 1764, Jefferson came into the inheritance from his father, which included land in Charlottesville, Virginia, and the "little mountain." Soon Jefferson filled his notebooks with plans and dreams for a house that he named Monticello (pronounced *Montichello*), Italian for "little mountain."

According to William Short, a friend and later Jefferson's secretary, Jefferson acquired his first architecture book from an old cabinetmaker near the college gate. After reading it, he became infatuated with the design and building of structures. Jefferson could see that there were rules in architecture just as there were rules in nature. He read as many architecture books from England as he could find, but there were few. In the colonies, there were no architects who designed houses. Pioneers built their own homes, usually with the help of family members and slaves.

To Jefferson, the mansions and wooden frame houses looked "ordinary" compared to the classical style of ancient Greek and Roman buildings. When he read Andrea Palladio's *Four Books of Architecture*, he was influenced by the artistic designs of that famous Italian architect. From his father, Jefferson had learned how to draw with ink like a draftsman. Possessing this talent, he designed his magnificent home, Monticello, creating a new

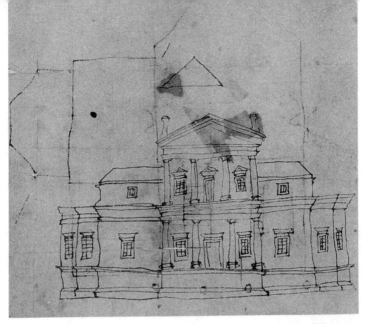

*Thomas Jefferson's first drawing of Monticello.*

style of building that had not been seen before in America.

At home in the summer of 1765, Jefferson's sister Martha was making plans for her wedding. Jefferson was delighted when he found that his sister was marrying his dear school friend, Dabney Carr. But not long after that happy occasion, sorrow touched his life again. His older sister Jane became ill and died at age twenty-five. Jefferson remembered how Jane had taken care of him at Tuckahoe, sang songs as he played the fiddle, and listened to his plans for the future. He would miss her very much.

In 1767 Thomas Jefferson was admitted to the bar of Virginia's General Court by his mentor and friend, George Wythe. Jefferson then began to practice law before the General Court in Williamsburg, building a reputation for himself as a fine lawyer. He also visited other courts in the counties to meet with prospective clients. He practiced law until the Revolutionary War later caused the courts to close.

Jefferson was glad his work gave him time at home to supervise farm activities and help his mother, brother, and sisters. He wished to design his own garden and in a garden notebook wrote, "1767 Mar. 23. Purple Hyacinth and Narcissus bloom. Apr. 2. Sowed Carnations, Indian pink, Marygold . . . Cayenne pepper."

# 3
## *Lawyer and Lawmaker*
## *1767–1775*

**B**y 1768 Thomas Jefferson was well-known in the county as a successful lawyer and planter. His political career began when the landowners of Albemarle County elected him as one of their representatives to the Virginia House of Burgesses in Williamsburg.

Although Williamsburg's population was less than 2000 people, the city was the capital and commercial center of the colony of Virginia. Here the colonists found education, religion, politics, government, militia, and social life. The main street, Duke of Gloucester, was a dirt road covered with layers of sand and powdered oyster shells to try to keep it less muddy in winter. The road led from the College of William and Mary past a few hundred houses to the capitol, with the brick Bruton

Parish Church halfway, at the intersection of Palace Green.

During "Publick Times," when the courts were in session, the country town more than doubled its size to a mini-metropolis. Horse-drawn carriages clopped up and down Duke of Gloucester with visitors on the way to the capitol, the Governor's Palace, and the taverns, for dinners, parties, and balls. In the government courts, regulations were passed regarding tobacco, land grants, Indian trade, and the settlement of immigrants in new cities. Indian tribesmen were familiar visitors to the capital.

*In his journals, Jefferson documented customs of Native Americans like these three Cherokee Chiefs.*

Walking along brick sidewalks, gentlemen doffed their three-cornered hats and bowed to friends on their way to the bootmaker's, the gunsmith's, or the wigmaker's. The ladies might be found shopping at a milliner's for frills and finery, or the silversmith's for a gleaming candleholder, or purchasing baskets woven of oak splits.

When the crowds left, the town was returned to its usual group of inhabitants: officials of the government and county, professors and students from the college, and a large group of people who maintained the inns, taverns, eating houses, and public houses, or saloons. Close by were merchants and artisans, doctors and lawyers.

On Sundays, the colonists attended Bruton Parish Church. Church and state were united in Virginia, and the colonists could not choose their religion or change their laws. All officeholders were required to attend the Anglican church regularly. In order to serve as a member of the government, a person had to be approved by the minister of the Church of England.

The governor's pew, with its canopied chair, was reserved for royal governors and council members. Church members sat in high boxlike pews, small enclosures with a door to keep out the cold and drafts in the unheated church. Four United States presidents worshipped there during their terms of office: George Washington, Thomas Jefferson, James Monroe, and John Tyler.

The South Gallery was reserved for speakers of the House of Burgesses and the college faculty.

Students at William and Mary were required to attend church every Sunday. During the two- to three-hour church service, the boys were known to carve their initials, and the markings are still evident on the handrail in the West Gallery.

The colony's highest royal tribunal, the General Court, made up of the governor and his counsel, met in the spring and fall to try cases and pass judgment. Punishment was severe for debtors and common criminals. In the Public Gaol (pronounced *jail*), minor offenders suffered discomfort and ridicule on the outdoor pillory and stocks. Common criminals were held inside the brick building with leg irons, handcuffs, and chains, waiting to be tried.

The King's Council and the General Assembly of the House of Burgesses also met twice a year in the state capital. The first representatives of the colonists did not hesitate to challenge their governors and to assume new powers of their own. The colonists felt they deserved more freedom to govern themselves because they had cleared, settled, and developed the land.

As one of the burgesses, Jefferson often met with other colonial leaders in the Apollo Room at the Raleigh Tavern to discuss their problems. One of them was the orator and statesman Patrick Henry. In 1765, when Jefferson was studying law, he had been impressed by Henry's fiery speech against the Stamp Act. The act had passed, imposing the first direct tax by the English Parliament on the thirteen American colonies.

*Patrick Henry stands up in the Virginia House of Burgesses to denounce Britain's Stamp Bill.*

*Rioters in New York protest the Stamp Act.*

The revenue stamps — required on all news-papers, pamphlets, playing cards, and docu-ments — helped to finance the British Army stationed in America. Many people in the colonies protested against the tax and boycotted English goods. In Williamsburg, the Stamp Act provoked a mob scene in front of a coffee house, as angry colonists cried out against "taxation without rep-resentation." The boycott finally led Parliament to repeal the Stamp Act a year later.

At Shadwell, Jefferson watched over the work on Monticello as it slowly progressed. In 1768 and 1769 the top of "little mountain" was cleared and leveled. Then Jefferson ordered the digging of a cellar and a well. Thousands of bricks were made by hand, and lumber was cut from trees. Slaves gathered stone and limestone that was quarried on Jefferson's land. In 1770, construction began on the first structure, an 18' × 18' outbuilding called the South Pavilion.

One day without warning, a fire broke out at Shadwell and Jane Jefferson's frame house burned to the ground. Jefferson wrote his friend John Page that his mother was safe, but the fire burned "every paper I had in the world and almost every book." The servants saved his fiddle, and Jefferson had a few books that were on loan to friends. In one of them, his "Garden Book," begun in 1766, he had listed planting dates, names of plants, and blooms. And he continued to record them over a period of fifty-eight years.

Jefferson was keeping bachelor quarters in the South Pavilion when he met Martha Wayles Skelton. It is probable that Jefferson first courted her in Williamsburg, when she was there for the social season. It is known that in the fall of 1770, Jefferson sent his slave Jupiter to buy new shoe buckles, hair powder, and many tickets for plays.

Martha was a young heiress, and already a widow. Of slender figure, with hazel eyes and auburn hair, she was pretty and talented. Martha and Thomas shared a love of music and enjoyed playing duets together. Martha was accomplished on the harpsichord and pianoforte, and Jefferson on the violin and cello.

On New Year's Day 1772, Martha and Thomas were married at the bride's plantation home, The Forest, near Williamsburg. After traveling almost to Monticello through a driving snowstorm, they found that their carriage could go no farther through the snow. The couple decided to push on by horseback the last eight miles to reach their honeymoon cottage. Arriving late at night, they found the servants asleep. Jefferson built a fire and looked around for something to eat or drink. Finding a leftover half-bottle of wine, they toasted their new home with song and laughter. The South Pavilion became the newlyweds' one-room parlor, bedchamber, and study, with a kitchen below.

In September their happiness increased when Martha gave birth to their first child, a daughter named Martha, who was called Patsy. Jefferson kept busy with his home, planning the gardens and farmland. Room by room, the main house was completed over a period of ten years. When Jefferson was away, Martha and Patsy received letters from him.

At that time, written messages were an important means of communication. In March of 1773, Jefferson, along with his brother-in-law Dabney Carr and other burgesses, urged the formation of Committees of Correspondence in the colonies. The committees were to write letters showing their sympathy and support to the people of Boston, and Massachusetts, especially their tea merchants, who were suffering because of Britain's tax on tea.

A month later at Charlottesville, thirty-year-old

Dabney Carr was taken ill with bilious fever and the doctor could not save him. Jefferson remembered their boyhood days and his promise to Carr. Within the week he ordered a graveyard cleared and a grave dug beneath their favorite oak tree on "little mountain."

After Carr's death, Jefferson managed the Carr family's affairs, taking care of his sister Martha, her son Peter, and baby Martha, in addition to his own family. A month later, another sorrowful event occurred. Jefferson's father-in-law, the well-known attorney John Wayles, passed away. Martha Jefferson inherited a considerable portion of his estate.

The following year, Monticello's middle building was near completion, and the vegetable garden and vineyard were planted. Martha was expecting her second child and Jefferson stayed close to her. On April 3, Martha gave birth to Jane Randolph Jefferson.

The news from England was not good. The British Parliament had passed harsh decrees against the colonists. Beginning with the Townshend Acts of 1767, the laws had suspended the Massachusetts assembly and imposed duties on lead, glass, paint, paper, and tea. The colonists had responded by saying that they would not buy or import any goods taxed by Parliament, and in 1770 Parliament repealed the duties, except the tax on tea.

Bostonians especially objected to the presence of British soldiers in Boston. Colonists were enraged when a group of soldiers fired on a taunting mob, killing and injuring unarmed people in what became known as the Boston Massacre.

But protests were of no avail. The tea tax and other restrictions hurt the colonies. In December of 1773, at what came to be called the Boston Tea Party, colonial patriots boarded three East India Company ships and tossed 342 casks of tea into Boston Harbor. To punish the dissenters, the British Parliament passed five laws in 1774, which the colonists called the "Intolerable Acts." The laws suspended many of the colonists' original rights, and closed Boston Harbor to trade.

In May 1774, when the assembly met, the House of Burgesses objected loudly to the laws that ordered the closing of Boston's port. Lord Dunmore, for the third time, dissolved the yearly meeting of the House of Burgesses. Jefferson wrote in his autobiography, "We retired to the Apollo, as before, agreed to an association, and instructed the committee of correspondence to propose to the corresponding committees of other colonies to appoint deputies to meet in Congress at such place, *annually*, as should be convenient, to direct from time to time the measures required by the general interest, and we declared that an attack on any one colony should be considered as an attack on the whole."

On June 1, the day that the port of Boston was closed, a day of fasting and solemn prayer was called across the colonies. Jefferson had originated the idea that colonists gather in parish churches and pray to avoid the evils of civil war. He hoped the religious observance would influence the powerful Church of England to intercede in their behalf.

In July, the freeholders in all the counties of Virginia reelected the same members of the original assembly of the House of Burgesses to act as delegates at a Virginia convention in August.

As one of the delegates, Jefferson wrote resolutions in reply to the Intolerable Acts. On his way by horseback to deliver them, he became ill on the road with dysentery. This was the only time in his life when he could not attend to a public duty because of illness. He asked Jupiter to take the papers safely to the chairman, Peyton Randolph. One copy was to be delivered to Randolph and the other to Patrick Henry. Jefferson hoped they would be approved as instructions to the Virginia delegates to Congress, accepted by the members of the Continental Congress in Philadelphia, then addressed to the king.

Jefferson's resolutions were published as a pamphlet called *A Summary View of the Rights of British America*. In it Jefferson pointed out that the colonists had conquered and settled the wilds of the New World without the aid of Britain. Therefore, he argued that the exercise of free trade was a natural right of the colonists. Jefferson denied the authority of the English Parliament over the colonies' right to govern themselves. His views were bold and fervent, expressing the ideals that he would write later in the Declaration of Independence.

In September 1774, at the First Continental Congress, every colony was represented except Georgia. In the midst of heated debate, many argued for reconciliation. Jefferson hoped the Congress would adopt his resolutions, but it did not. Some thought the pamphlet inflammatory, yet Jefferson's ideas remained in the minds of the delegates. The members drew up a Declaration of Grievances, which demanded the repeal of some thirteen laws. But the British Parliament and King George III refused to do so.

Originally the colonists had chosen to continue their union with the mother country. However, the increasingly severe measures taken by Britain were widely protested throughout the colonies. In March of 1775, the burgesses from the Virginia colonies convened again in a neutral place, in Richmond, Virginia. Thomas Jefferson was there, representing Albemarle County. It was at Old Saint John's Church that Patrick Henry uttered his famous words, "Give me liberty or give me death." Jefferson must have cheered enthusiastically, for he was a strong supporter of Patrick Henry's resolutions.

Fearful of British attack, people started to arm themselves. In April, British Regulars fired against colonial militiamen. With what became known as "the shot heard round the world," the Revolutionary War began. After the bloody battles of Lex-

*Revolutionary troops battle British redcoats in the Battle of Lexington.*

ington and Concord, the colonial representatives knew the meeting of the Second Continental Congress would be very important.

Before the First Continental Congress had adjourned, Jefferson had been elected as an alternate delegate to attend the Second Continental Congress, in place of Peyton Randolph. But he did not believe that he had a chance of going. However, at the last moment, Lord Dunmore sent for Randolph. The governor had decided to hold another assembly of the House of Burgesses to consider a new conciliatory proposal from Lord North, Prime Minister of Great Britain. As speaker of the House, Randolph could not refuse to be present.

Jefferson was now the delegate to attend the Second Continental Congress on June 22 in Philadelphia. He returned home to tell his wife the exciting news, then decided it was best for Martha and the children to stay at The Forest while he was gone. Before Jefferson left, Peyton Randolph prevailed upon him to stop in Williamsburg to prepare the reply to Lord North's proposal.

Peyton Randolph believed Jefferson to be the most effective writer in America. And indeed, history was about to be made at the Second Continental Congress. There Jefferson would reveal to the world his skill as a writer and statesman.

# 4
# The Declaration
# of Independence
# 1775–1776

It took Jefferson ten days to ride the 250 miles from Monticello to Williamsburg and then to Philadelphia. The city's population of around 50,000 was much larger than most others in the colonies. There were people from all walks of life, some fashionably dressed men and women, others militiamen, patriots, loyalists, and messenger boys who were hurrying to deliver important documents. When Jefferson found an apartment in the noisy city, he paid a "fortnight's lodging for self and servant 3-15." [3 pounds, 15 shillings.] The horses cost more to board than his room did.

On June 22, 1775, Jefferson entered the red colonial State House on Chestnut Street, later known as Independence Hall. In the yard, newly formed battalions of Philadelphia soldiers practiced their drills. Inside the conference room, behind locked doors, the delegates suffered from the intense summer heat. A few annoying flies entered through the slightly open high windows. Jefferson had been unsure of his welcome, but he was greeted warmly by the delegates. He was glad to meet John Adams of Massachusetts, a fine debater, lawyer, and leader of the radicals. The two men would become good friends. Jefferson also had looked forward to meeting Benjamin Franklin. Dr. Franklin had just returned from England and knew the government's policies.

One problem that demanded immediate action was the war effort. The delegates had already called for a Continental army to defend the colonies, and later appointed George Washington the Commander in Chief. Thomas Jefferson greatly admired this strong leader of the Continental forces.

The Congress immediately recognized Jefferson's quick, decisive ways and appointed him to a committee. Along with John Dickinson and others, he wrote the Declaration of the Causes and Necessity for Taking up Arms. After the committee revised the declaration, only four and a half paragraphs of Jefferson's original composition appeared in the final draft. But the words he wrote for Washington's men helped them understand why they were fighting the British. Jefferson said, "We fight not for glory or for conquest. . . . We fight in defense of the freedom that is our birthright. . . ."

At the end of July, Jefferson penned another

reply to Lord North, an official refusal from the Congress, regarding North's so-called "conciliatory" proposals. Congress adjourned during the hot month of August, and Jefferson was appointed to be a regular delegate to the Second Continental Congress in Philadelphia on September 5. The other delegates appointed from Virginia were Peyton Randolph, George Wythe, Richard Henry Lee, Francis Lightfoot Lee, and two friends of Jefferson's from William and Mary, Benjamin Harrison and Thomas Nelson, Jr.

Before leaving for Monticello, Jefferson said good-bye to his cousin John Randolph, who had decided to return home to England. Jefferson told him his real home was Virginia. Unlike Randolph's brother Peyton and son Edmund, who were patriots, John disagreed with their ideas of liberty.

Jefferson asked Randolph to intercede with King George III and the British ministry, telling them the true state of affairs in the colonies. He would miss his cousin and the time they spent together, enjoying music. Before he left, Randolph sold Jefferson the beautiful Italian violin he had always wanted.

On the way home from Philadelphia, Jefferson decided to stop in Richmond to catch up on local news. The Virginia Convention had become the revolutionary government of Virginia, but Jefferson's colleagues still hoped that their disagreements with Britain could be solved peacefully. It wasn't until the following year that they actually believed in *fighting* for the cause of freedom.

Jefferson had already turned over his law practice to his young cousin, Edmund Randolph. Now at home in Monticello, he acted as husband and landowner, helping Martha with the house and children, and running the plantation. Content to be there, he could spend more time with his dear wife. Martha seemed delicate and he worried about her.

Early September 1775, their baby Jane died, only seventeen months old. Martha could not be consoled. Thomas stayed with her as long as he could, missing the opening of Congress. Finally he decided to take Martha and three-year-old Patsy to Eppington to stay with Elizabeth Eppes, Martha's half sister. Hustling the horses all the way, Jefferson arrived in Philadelphia six days later, on September 25.

One evening shortly after his arrival, Jefferson and Peyton Randolph were dining with a friend in one of the taverns. Suddenly Peyton had a fatal stroke (then called "apoplexy"). Jefferson was shocked to lose his cousin, whom he so admired and respected.

Usually Jefferson set aside one day every week to write letters. He wrote Martha about Peyton, but she did not answer. Instead, he received a letter from Elizabeth's husband, Francis Eppes, saying that Martha was still very depressed after the loss of her last baby. She was in no mood to write or do much else, either.

In Philadelphia, Congress had asked again for a peaceful settlement with Britain, demanding only their "rights" as Englishmen. But by the end of the year, the colonists changed their opinions to demands for independence. There were skirmishes and scattered fighting along the East Coast. Early in November of 1775, Lord Dunmore declared martial law in Virginia, and on January 1, 1776, he ordered Norfolk set on fire, and it burned to the ground. The same thing happened at Falmouth, Maine.

Jefferson hurried home to Monticello, where his family now was, to be sure they were far enough away from the fighting. He found his family safe. The servants had just built a deer park, and the children were fascinated with the soft creatures that they could touch and feed.

In the completed dining room, Martha, Thomas, and the family enjoyed suppers during the late afternoon before the daylight hours disappeared. Although there was a fireplace, the dining room and adjoining tearoom were the coldest rooms in the house. Years later, Jefferson installed double doors between the two rooms, closing off the tearoom in the wintertime. He also installed a revolving door with shelves so servants bringing food from the kitchen did not need to enter the dining room. Jefferson was very creative and liked to experiment with gadgets to improve his home. Many of his later ideas came from his travels in Europe.

Some of Jefferson's duties while he was home took him into the counties to collect money for the poor in Boston and also for the purchase of gunpowder for the Virginia militia. Jefferson kept writing letters and received news from friends in Williamsburg and Philadelphia.

He learned that Lord Dunmore had removed the colonists' gunpowder from the storage magazine in Williamsburg in April, and placed it on a British schooner in the James River. Patrick Henry had led an angry group from Hanover to get the powder back. He did not succeed, but obtained its value in money.

Lord Dunmore called an assembly meeting, so Jefferson left for Williamsburg. During the Virginia assembly, the burgesses showed so much anger questioning the governor about his actions, that he was afraid and took flight with his family to the man-of-war *Fowey* on the river. From there he tried, not very successfully, to conduct the Crown's business at a distance.

It was January 1776, and Jefferson was home again. His friend Tom Nelson had sent him a copy of the pamphlet *Common Sense* by Thomas Paine. In it, Paine attacked the British monarch and urged the American colonists to declare independence. Paine's writings originated from ideas about God, reason, and nature that were circulating in Europe in the seventeenth and eighteenth centuries, the period known as the Age of Reason.

On March 31, 1776, Jane Randolph Jefferson suffered a stroke and died suddenly at the age of fifty-seven. Jefferson was heartsick over the death of his mother and was ill with "the head ach" that lasted several weeks.

In late May, the Continental Congress voted that "every kind of authority under the Crown should be totally suppressed," and they asked the states to set up independent governments. Jefferson, accompanied by Jupiter, rode to Philadelphia. Tucked away safely in his money pouch were the funds he had collected for gunpowder and relief for the poor.

Again he took lodgings with Benjamin Randolph on Chestnut Street. Jefferson knew Randolph was a fine cabinetmaker and asked him to build a unique folding writing box for him, using his directions. The desk had a drawer that could be locked, a place for supplies of ink, nibs (points for a quill pen), and sand for blotting. The writing desk was made from a beautiful piece of mahogany.

*The desk on which the Declaration of Independence was written, from a drawing by Jefferson.*

*Thomas Jefferson wrote the Declaration in this house.*

Jefferson was looking for a cooler and quieter place to work, and after eight days of searching he rented the second floor of a brick house in another section of Philadelphia.

In June of 1776 at the State House, the Second Continental Congress decided to draw up a written declaration of independence from England. They must explain to the world why the colonies wanted to separate from their mother country. Virginia delegate Richard Henry Lee had received instructions from the convention at Williamsburg to prepare a declaration of independence. On June 7, Lee introduced three resolutions calling for in-

*The Declaration writing committee:* (left to right) *Thomas Jefferson, Roger Sherman, Benjamin Franklin, Robert R. Livingston, and John Adams.*

dependence, foreign alliances with other nations, and unity in a confederation.

The Congress postponed the final vote until July 1 in order to give the delegates time to debate the issues, as some states were under instructions to vote against them. Meanwhile, Congress appointed a committee to draft the declaration, just in case it was passed.

Thomas Jefferson was chosen as the leading member of the five-man committee, which included Benjamin Franklin, John Adams, Robert R. Livingston, and Roger Sherman. Although one of the youngest of the men, Jefferson was asked to do the actual writing because of his literary skill and knowledge of democratic principles. The committee felt his words would be plain, firm, and concise, expressing their purpose.

Jefferson isolated himself in his second-floor parlor and bedroom for seventeen days, following a strict routine. He got up as soon as it was daylight and soaked his feet in a basin of cold water, which he believed helped to ward off colds. After playing his violin, he worked on the declaration, writing on his lap top desk in the parlor.

Sometimes he wrote standing up, by candlelight. His quill pen scratched out words and revised them constantly to make the composition easier to understand. What he wrote came from his own thoughts, from what he had read, from philosophers and historians, and from ideas discussed with friends. Over the years, he had kept important remarks copied down in his commonplace books. Now all his studies, knowledge, and talent were put to the test.

Jefferson believed that *people* form governments, and governments get their power from the *people*. He explained that the colonies were no longer bound to England and wrote that ". . . all Men are created equal, that they are endowed by their Creator with certain unalienable Rights, that among these are Life, Liberty, and the pursuit of Happiness."

When the declaration was finished, one copy was made for John Adams, and another sent by messenger to Dr. Franklin. The draft, which was almost all Jefferson's own work, was submitted to

A Declaration by the Representatives of the UNITED STATES OF AMERICA, in General Congress assembled.

When in the course of human events it becomes necessary for one people to dissolve the political bands which have connected them with another, and to ~~[as~~ assume among the powers of the earth the *separate and equal* station to which the laws of nature & of nature's god entitle them, a decent respect to the opinions of mankind requires that they should declare the causes which impel them to the *the* separation.

We hold these truths to be *self-evident:* that all men are created equal; that *they are endowed by their creator with* certain *inherent &* inalienable rights; that among these are life, & liberty, & the pursuit of happiness; that to secure these *rights,* governments are instituted among men, deriving their just powers from the consent of the governed; that whenever any form of government becomes destructive of these ends, it is the right of the people to alter or to abolish it, & to institute new government, laying it's foundation on such principles & organising it's powers in such form, as to them shall seem most likely to effect their safety & happiness. prudence indeed will dictate that governments long established should not be changed for light & transient causes: and accordingly all experience hath shewn that mankind are more disposed to suffer while evils are sufferable, than to right themselves by abolishing the forms to which they are accustomed but

*A draft of the Declaration in Jefferson's own handwriting.*

51

Congress on June 28, with only minor changes.

During the meetings of the Congress, when others criticized the declaration and tried to revise it, Jefferson kept silent. John Adams kept jumping to his feet, arguing against any change. Ben Franklin tried to comfort his young colleague, who felt his composition was being damaged by alterations. Many of Jefferson's original remarks were dropped, but most of the brilliant writing remained.

It is interesting that Jefferson, the slave owner, had included a section that condemned slavery. However, that part was thrown out because some states would have refused to sign the declaration if the section remained. Also, Congress reworded the second to last paragraph to include words of Richard Henry Lee's resolutions. On July 2, 1776, Congress passed the resolution affirming that the states were independent of the British Crown.

On July 4, Jefferson arose at dawn as usual. He noted in the back of his account book that the temperature was 68 degrees Fahrenheit. From then on, he decided that he would keep a daily record of the weather, and after he reached the State House, he took the temperature again. The highest reading, at one o'clock, was 76 degrees.

This was the day that the Declaration of Independence was adopted by Congress. President of the Congress, John Hancock, signed the document with a flourish, followed by the secretary, Charles Thomson. On July 9, New York adopted a resolution supporting the declaration and became the

*Thomas Jefferson and the writing committee present the Declaration of Independence to John Hancock and the Continental Congress.*

thirteenth colony to approve. On July 15, the document was laid before Congress and became The Unanimous Declaration of the Thirteen United States of America.

Copies were sent to the officials of each colony and commanding officers of the Continental Army. It was read aloud at the head of each brigade of soldiers and in public places. It was celebrated in the public square with speeches, flags flying, and the fife and drum corps beating out patriotic songs.

But it was not until August 2 that the Declaration of Independence was finally lettered in parchment and signed by all the congressional members. Then the document was taken away and hidden in a secret place to safeguard the names of the dedicated men who had signed it.

The names were not released for six months. The British had said all traitors would be hanged. If the revolution failed, the signers and their families would be found, homes looted, farms and businesses destroyed, and the signers would suffer a traitor's death.

Today, that inspired piece of paper on which a mighty nation was founded is on display for the public in the National Archives Building in Washington, D.C. Its simple, elegant, and forceful words still inspire speeches, flags flying, and bands playing every Fourth of July.

# 5
# *Virginia Laws:*
# *A Single Eye to Reason*
# *1777–1779*

**N**ow that the Declaration of Independence had been adopted, the Continental Congress acted as the colonies' first government. John Adams and the legislators began a draft of the Articles of Confederation, a written document intended to unite the states.

Jefferson sat in the Congress every day, listening to debates and taking notes. He was especially concerned with how much money each state would contribute, and the number of votes allowed members of Congress. Jefferson believed that the states could do more for themselves than Congress could.

After their experience with Britain, the colonists were suspicious of remote government. On paper the Articles of Confederation gave the Congress power to regulate and control foreign and Indian affairs, the military, the monetary system, the postal service, and matters concerning interstate trade. Each state had one vote. In turn the Congress was dependent on the states for funds to carry out its decrees. But Jefferson could foresee that the Articles would be difficult to enforce, since they limited the states' powers.

Jefferson was anxious to get home to Martha, who was ill again. Although his request had been refused twice, he asked Congress to release him as a Virginia delegate. This time Congress agreed, but reminded him of his duties to the General Assembly in Williamsburg, where he had been re-elected to the House of Delegates.

However, Jefferson stayed in Philadelphia through the hot days of August. There was still work to be done with his friends Franklin and Adams on the design of the United States seal. He left Philadelphia on September 3, and traveled a shorter route home, reaching Monticello in six days.

The leaves were falling and the weather was a typical brisk autumn as the Jeffersons spent September together. Sometimes in the evening Martha and Thomas read to each other and enjoyed music. In the parlor was Martha's pianoforte, which had been shipped from England, Jefferson's gift to her when they were first married.

Construction of their home at Monticello was still in progress, with workmen busy laying brick and preparing the woodwork. The men were housed in a small dwelling on Mulberry Row, named for the mulberry trees planted there. This 1,000-foot-long road became the center of plantation activity in the 1770s. Eventually there would be nineteen buildings on the site, including dwellings for both black and white workers, wood and ironworking shops, a smokehouse and dairy, a wash house, a storehouse, and a stable. Jefferson's slaves and employees used the shops to build carriages, furniture, and other equipment.

Along the contours of the slope, Jefferson had begun a vegetable garden. Salad was an important part of Jefferson's diet, and peas were his favorite vegetable. The gardens were like a laboratory, where over the years Jefferson experimented with 250 varieties of vegetables and herbs.

Seeds arrived from abroad: squash and broccoli from Italy, peppers from Mexico, fifteen types of English pea, and as many as twenty varieties of bean. Jefferson even ate tomatoes, although at that time the rest of the country thought they were poisonous.

In October 1776, when the House of Delegates met again, Jefferson returned to Williamsburg. He was delighted his wife felt well enough to go with him. George Wythe had offered his home as a place for the couple to stay, the same home where Jefferson had once studied law.

At the beginning of the session, the House of Delegates approved the preparation of two bills. On October 12, Jefferson introduced one of the bills that called for the general revision of the Virginia code of laws. He was convinced that the code "should be corrected in all its parts, with a single eye to reason, and the good of those for whose government it was framed." The report was called the "Revisal."

On October 14, Jefferson introduced the second bill, which opposed the law called "entail." Originally all property of the estate was inherited by family members "entail" from generation to generation. Jefferson's new law would break up the vast landholdings that kept the power and prestige with the aristocracy.

The lawmaker wanted to give all members of society a chance to advance, and he pictured many communities of individual farmers, each cultivating their own land across the immense country. Those without property were to be given fifty acres, and squatters would receive grants in small quantities in outlying areas.

Edmund Pendleton, speaker of the House, had led the opposition to Jefferson's bill. Others sided with Pendleton, but the law against entails passed within a month. The landed gentry hated Jefferson for these changes. Jefferson felt his work on the Virginia laws was vital to carry out the ideals expressed in the Declaration of Independence.

During his writing of the "Revisal," Jefferson prepared an attack against a related law known as "primogeniture." The English primogeniture law stated that property descended intact to the eldest son in the family from generation to generation, without an inheritance for other sons or daughters.

Jefferson's bill "authorized the present holder to divide the property among his children equally, as his affections were divided, and would place them, by natural generation on the level of their fellow citizens."

It took another nine years before the old primogeniture law was abolished in the Virginia legislature. Jefferson's land reforms were part of a movement that abolished primogeniture and entail in practically all of the states within ten years of the Declaration of Independence.

It would take almost three years, from 1776 to 1779, to prepare the bills that revised Virginia's code of law. The House had appointed Jefferson as chairman of a five-man committee, with George Mason, Thomas Ludwell Lee, Edmund Pendleton, and George Wythe. Their instructions were to revise, repeal, and amend the present laws, or introduce other bills, making them clear and understandable. Jefferson was glad to have his mentor, attorney George Wythe, on the committee.

After the House of Delegates adjourned in the fall of 1776, Jefferson and Martha went home again. The lawmaker began reading books in his library. Some he had collected from professors and lawyer friends, others were rare volumes of Virginia manuscripts, old laws, and the newspapers. Jefferson worked long and diligently at his task.

In January of 1777, only three revisors met in Fredericksburg to discuss the revision of Virginia's laws. Mason and Lee had disqualified themselves from drafting statutes because they were not lawyers. Jefferson was made responsible for the English statutes passed before 1607, Wythe undertook the common law passed after the founding of Virginia, and Edmund Pendleton reviewed laws passed only in the Virginia colony. The lawmakers worked separately, sending letters to each other when the House was not in session. Letters also arrived from members of Congress informing Jefferson about affairs of the Commonwealth and on the Continent.

Besides his public work as a delegate and revisor, Jefferson was a county lieutenant. He pre-

*General Washington and the Marquis de Lafayette visit wounded soldiers at Valley Forge.*

pared the paperwork for the militia, and served as an Albemarle magistrate. During the severe winter, Patrick Henry wrote to Jefferson appointing him county collector, assigned to collect blankets and rugs for the freezing soldiers in New Jersey. At the same time, George Washington and the Continental Army dug in at Valley Forge for the coldest winter ever.

At Monticello during a terrible chill, the wells dried up and water had to be dragged from a spring on the side of the mountain up the winding road. Martha was not feeling well again and expected another baby in the spring.

In May of 1777, when the delegates met, Jefferson stayed only sixteen days of the eight-week session. He was given a leave of absence again to be with Martha. On May 28, Martha gave birth to their only son. The happiness turned to sorrow when the baby died seventeen days later. In Jefferson's pocket diary he noted under June 14, "Our son died 10 h. 20m. pm." Jefferson could be found at Martha's side, or working late at night by the light of the oil lamp, trying to overcome his grief.

In May of the next year, when their daughter Patsy was almost six years old, Martha gave birth to a baby girl. Martha named her Mary; Jefferson called her Polly. He did not leave Martha or the baby for the fall assembly until he was sure they were both feeling strong.

That year had been another busy time of planting and building on the mountaintop. New trees were added to the orchard: plum, pear, cherry, apple, quince, apricot, and bitter almond. The master of Monticello recorded that 90,000 bricks were made, and in one summer month 14,000 bricks were laid for new buildings.

At Monticello, Jefferson was absorbed with the difficult task of revising the laws. In the colonies the Revolutionary War continued, with victories and defeats on both sides. Early in the war, the assembly had split into two groups: Tories, who were loyal to the king, and Whigs, who favored liberty for the colonies. Tories fought alongside the British soldiers, together with mercenaries— those men willing to fight on either side for pay.

During Jefferson's time at home, John Adams wrote him, "We want your industry and abilities here extremely. Your country is not yet quite secure enough to excuse your retreat to the delights of domestic life."

Finally, in February of 1779, the revisors met for the last time, in Williamsburg. Jefferson wrote, "Meeting day by day, we examined critically our several parts, sentence by sentence, scrutinizing and amending, until we had agreed on the whole." Jefferson and Wythe prepared much of the final revision and presented it to the assembly in June. By then, both Pendleton and Wythe had been appointed judges and Jefferson elected governor.

The lawmakers hardly noticed the revisions and new bills, because their great concern was the Revolutionary War. But Jefferson's bills became the foundation for many humane laws that would be passed later.

Looking back on this time, Jefferson felt the years from 1776 to 1779 were his most rewarding and productive. In his book, *Notes on Virginia*, penned in 1781, he wrote about the changes he had proposed. Four bills were of special interest to him, those concerning education, slavery, religious freedom, and crime and punishment.

Jefferson believed that no democracy could survive without public education. His bill for "the More General Diffusion of Knowledge" proposed the establishment of a public school system for children throughout the state. Jefferson's bill also included sections amending the constitution of the College of William and Mary, and establishing a public library in Richmond. The bill was not enacted until the end of the century, and then it was a diluted version.

In 1776 Jefferson had wanted to end the slave trade. He urged passage of a bill in 1778 that outlawed the importation of slaves into the state and noted that half of Virginia's total population were slaves. He favored gradual emancipation. If his act had passed, all slaves would have been freed, remained with their parents, and been trained at public expense for useful employment. When reaching maturity, blacks would have been colonized in other parts of the growing country.

To Jefferson, freedom for slaves also meant protecting them. He questioned the abilities of the black race, but his mind remained open. Years later, he corresponded with a black mathemati-

*A letter from Jefferson to scientist Benjamin Bannecker.*

cian named Benjamin Bannecker, whom he considered "very respectable."

Although he kept slaves himself, Jefferson believed that slavery was fundamentally cruel. In his *Notes on Virginia*, he spoke of the "unremitting despotism" on the part of slave owners and "degrading submission" on the part of slaves. "Our children see this and learn to imitate it," he wrote.

After the revolution began, Jefferson noticed that people were changing their attitudes about slavery. And in 1778, when he was away from the House, a successful measure passed to outlaw the importation of slaves into Virginia.

Another bill that Jefferson drafted in the House

of Delegates was an act for religious freedom. It was the most bitterly contested of his entire life. Jefferson felt very strongly that church and state should be separated, and he regarded religion as a strictly private affair. Because Jefferson respected the opinions of others, he was tolerant of other forms of religious worship. He asked that dissenters to the established Anglican church be exempt from taxes to support it.

The Freedom of Religion bill was not introduced until Jefferson became governor, and seven more years passed before it was enacted in 1786. Jefferson felt that it was the most important work of the revisors. Next to the Declaration of Independence, he considered it one of his greatest achievements.

In another part of the "Revisal," Jefferson asked that the death penalty, used freely against horse thieves and minor felons, be abolished except for murder and treason. There was fierce opposition to this bill and it did not pass. It was not until 1796 that the assembly adopted a bill limiting capital punishment.

Many of Jefferson's ideas were far ahead of his time. The Virginia legislature debated for a period of ten years before the Revisal bills became law. It was through the efforts of James Madison, who continually argued and prodded the members of the Continental Congress to pass Jefferson's bills, that many succeeded.

By 1786, of the 126 original bills submitted to the General Assembly, 56 amended bills had been

considered and passed. The remainder were referred to a new committee and eventually were
revised and enacted. In *Notes on Virginia* Jefferson
wrote, "It can never be too often repeated that the
time for fixing every essential right on a legal basis
is while our leaders are honest and ourselves
united."

In 1777 and 1778 the war came closer to Jefferson and his family. American General Horatio
Gates and his army had defeated British General
John Burgoyne at Saratoga, New York. It was a
decisive battle, for it brought France into the war
as an ally of the United States. The captured soldiers were British and also professional German

*General Burgoyne surrenders to revolutionary forces at Saratoga.*

soldiers called Hessians, who had been hired by King George III to help fight against the rebellion. Congress ordered the prisoners to march nearly 700 miles from Boston to Albemarle County, from which point they would be sent to England. Then Congress decided to leave the men near Charlottesville, Virginia.

Housing and feeding 4000 soldiers was a problem, especially during the winter months when food was scarce and the barracks unfinished. Jefferson heard that the prisoners would be split up and moved elsewhere, and he discussed the situation at great length with Governor Patrick Henry. Jefferson argued and won his point to allow the prisoners to stay together and take care of themselves. The men finished the barracks, planted gardens, and raised poultry for their food.

The British and German officers rented plantations nearby, and they often visited the Jefferson family for an evening of music. Jefferson extended his hospitality, but avoided discussion of public matters. In a note of gratitude, British general Philips wrote him, "The great cause that divides our country is not to be decided by individual animosities. . . . An intention to make others happy is the surest way of being happy ourselves."

Almost a year after Polly was born, thirty-six-year-old Thomas Jefferson was elected as Virginia's governor. It was June 1, 1779, and the Revolutionary War had been raging for four years. With France on America's side and Spain threatening Britain, a British army in the South had roared through Florida and almost subdued Georgia. With Virginia colonists fearful of the coming attacks, Jefferson's friends had nominated him for the position. His chief opponent had been John Page, lieutenant governor under Patrick Henry.

But neither man really wanted the job of wartime governor.

# 6
# *Governor of Virginia: The Fight for Freedom 1779–1784*

In the fall of 1779, when Martha felt strong enough, the family moved to the elegant Governor's Palace in Williamsburg. The Palace served as executive mansion for Patrick Henry and Thomas Jefferson, Virgina's first and second elected governors of the Commonwealth. In the entrance hall, the ceiling and walls held a display of swords, pistols, and muskets symbolizing the authority and might of the British Crown. Over 1600 items, beautiful pieces of silver and glass, were stored in the pantry.

Martha was pleased to find a double-keyboard harpsichord in the Palace ballroom, and the children frolicked on spacious lawns and gardens that included a wonderful winding maze of holly hedges. In a nearby canal, fish were caught for dinner. Jefferson spent hours each day with his council, along with John Page, John Walker, and his new friend, James Madison. James Madison would one day be the fourth president of the United States.

Two months before Jefferson took office, the British fleet had anchored in Chesapeake Bay. The 2000 men sent ashore captured a strong fort and, without losing a man, opened a path across Virginia's Tidewater. At Virginia's western border, George Rogers Clark was fighting against the British-led Indian forays and needed more money and ammunition.

Jefferson asked for help from other states, but did not receive any. People questioned Jefferson's wisdom in supporting the "common cause." Many Virginia soldiers had died defending other states, while their own shores were unprotected.

In April of 1780, threatened by invasion from sea, the assembly moved the capital inland from coastal Williamsburg to Richmond. In June, Jefferson was elected for a second term as governor. When he learned of Charleston's surrender and Virginia's losses, he offered Washington a plan to speed up military information. Jefferson proposed a "line of expresses from hence to the neighborhood of their army . . . to give us information of their movements."

At the rented house in Richmond where the family stayed, Martha gave birth to another daughter, Lucy Elizabeth Jefferson, on November 3. Five months later on a rainy April 15, baby Lucy died. Martha was so stricken that Jefferson would not leave her even to go across the street to a meeting.

Early in 1781, Jefferson began his *Notes on Virginia*. The secretary of the French Legion, François Marbois, had written Jefferson on behalf of the French government asking specific questions about his native state. In answering his questions, Jefferson compiled the most scientific study in America at that time. He included the Natural Bridge of Virginia located on his property, a famous natural wonder. Jefferson had obtained a patent and.purchased it from the Crown.

During these frantic war months, the governor took time to befriend a young Virginian, James Monroe, who had fought under Washington. Monroe had returned home unsure of what he wanted to do. Jefferson started him on his legal career and directed his studies. Later he commissioned Monroe as a lieutenant colonel and sent him to find the southern army and report the situation.

Monroe wrote Jefferson, "Whatever I am . . . or may be in the future has greatly arose from your friendship." The friendship lasted many years between the two great leaders, and Monroe later became the fifth president of the United States.

Again, in January of 1781, a British fleet appeared in the Chesapeake. Jefferson tried to round up militia to oppose them, but had little success. With Richmond threatened by attack, the governor directed the removal of public records and stores, then rushed his wife and children off to Tuckahoe, just west of Richmond. He rode back furiously to discover Brigadier General Benedict Arnold and the redcoats marching down Richmond's Main Street. After burning the public buildings and tobacco warehouses, the soldiers marched back to their ship and sailed downriver to Portsmouth, Virginia, where they set up base.

Washington sent word that the Marquis de Lafayette was marching south with 1200 Continentals to Richmond, where military advisors agreed they should make a stand. On April 29, 1781, Jefferson's small band of militiamen were bolstered by the French soldiers. But British General Cornwallis was advancing to Richmond with 9000 men, and Lafayette's small force could not prevent a major attack.

At the May session, the assembly moved the government as quickly as possible from Richmond to Charlottesville, seventy-five miles away. Jefferson brought his family back to Monticello, hoping they would be safe there.

In letters, Jefferson begged Washington to come to Virginia, convinced that the general could arouse the militia to drive out the British. But Washington couldn't leave New Jersey, and Cornwallis tramped through Virginia, burning and looting, while Jefferson and Lafayette could do nothing about it.

As a wartime governor, most of Jefferson's efforts were directed at defending the state against British invasion. Limited by the Virginia constitution, Jefferson's authority was weak and so was the army. Jefferson couldn't tighten the military law, which enabled almost anyone to avoid the call to arms, or requisition horses and supplies. He also couldn't stop inflation, and prices soared.

On June 4, 1781, the day after Jefferson's second term as governor ended, armed troops under the command of Captain McLeod marched on Jefferson's beloved Monticello. The surprise raid was ordered by Colonel Banastre Tarleton specifically to capture the author of the Declaration of Independence.

Virginian Jack Jouett saw the British troops on their way to Charlottesville. He raced through the woods on his horse to warn Jefferson and his family just in time for them to attempt an escape. Several assembly members who were staying at Monticello hurried to Charlottesville, three miles away; however, seven officials were captured.

Martha and the children were rushed in a carriage to Blenheim, a friend's plantation. Jefferson waited until almost every person had gone. A family story tells how close to danger Jefferson came that afternoon. He rode up nearby Montalto, or ("high mountain,") now Brown's Mountain, and dismounted. Looking through his telescope, he saw no soldiers.

When he knelt down, Jefferson realized that somewhere he had dropped the sword he usually wore. He stayed to search for it, then looked through the telescope again. Charlottesville was swarming with dragoons, heavily armed mounted soldiers. Jefferson left without the sword, knowing that if he were caught, he would be hanged immediately. Five minutes after he left, Captain

McLeod and his troops rode up the mountain and found the sword where Jefferson had dropped it.

The British held Monticello for eighteen hours, yet the soldiers touched nothing except a few bottles of wine. Jefferson was not so lucky with his Elk Hill plantation, inherited from his father-in-law in Goochland County. There Lord Cornwallis destroyed crops, burned barns, and carried off slaves and horses, and the rest of the animals to feed his troops.

Jefferson decided to move his family to Poplar Forest, another property he had inherited, that was located in Bedford County, ninety miles from Monticello. One morning Jefferson was riding over the farm on Caractacus, his favorite horse. Suddenly the animal pitched him from the saddle and Jefferson fell to the ground. The fall was unexpected, for Jefferson was a strong and fearless rider. In his words, he was "disabled from riding on horseback" for many weeks.

On top of these unhappy events in 1781, Jefferson received a letter saying that George Nicholas, a delegate from Hanover County, had presented a bill in Virginia's House of Delegates to investigate Jefferson's conduct of the war and his flight from Monticello. Because many of the officials had fled also, Jefferson did not take the matter seriously. When Captain McLeod had come to capture him, Jefferson's term of office had expired, although no new governor had been appointed.

Jefferson was sure that Patrick Henry was behind the motion attempting to destroy him. Henry and others had changed their views to the conservative side because they felt Jefferson had not been effective as a progressive governor. When Jefferson demanded that Nicholas explain the charges, he denied making them, saying that he was only asking questions concerning the preparation for war or the lack of it. The assembly adjourned until fall.

After a week without a governor, Thomas Nelson, Jr., a friend of Jefferson's, was elected and Jefferson was asked to go abroad as a peace commissioner. Once again he declined. In the past he had refused primarily because of Martha's health. This time he said that he had to stay in Virginia to attend to an important matter. He felt that he had to prove that it was not the misconduct of public officials that produced the misfortunes of war in his state, but rather the lack of funds to conduct the war and the disobedience of citizens called to arms.

That summer, Jefferson continued to write *Notes on Virginia* and completed it by the end of the year. He heard alarming news that there was a move in the assembly to create a temporary dictator, that the crisis would justify such an action. Jefferson argued zealously that democracy could function very well, even in such an emergency, and the scheme was narrowly defeated.

On October 19, 1781, with French naval support, General Washington and his French and American forces defeated the British Army at Yorktown, Virginia. With General Cornwallis's surrender, the major fighting of the Revolutionary War ended.

*This Currier & Ives engraving depicts a member of Washington's staff on the steps of Independence Hall at midnight, October 23, 1791, announcing the surrender of Cornwallis.*

The thirteen North American colonies that belonged to Britain had gained their independence.

In early December, Jefferson was reelected to the House of Delegates. There he answered the charges against him. Nicholas and others had withdrawn most of the original charges and were not present. The legislature closed the matter by adopting a unanimous resolution: "That the sincere thanks of the General Assembly be given to our former Governor, Thomas Jefferson, Esq. for his impartial, upright, and attentive administration while in office . . . and mean by thus publically avowing this opinion, to obviate and remove all unmerited censure."

Jefferson spent the six months from the fall of 1781 to the spring of 1782 taking care of his wife and keeping her company as she waited for the birth of another baby. He declined his seat in the assembly two days before Martha gave birth, and received a letter warning of arrest if he did not appear. Jefferson wrote James Monroe explaining his anxiety for Martha and was excused from duty.

On May 8, Martha gave birth to Lucy Elizabeth II, named after the little girl who had died. The strain of bearing so many children had weakened his wife dangerously. Jefferson was in torment over Martha's frail condition. He stayed at her bedside and read to her. His sister Martha Carr and sister-in-law Elizabeth Eppes were in the house, but Jefferson did most of the nursing. He was never out of calling distance. When he was not beside her, he was writing in a small room located near her bed.

On September 6, Martha Jefferson passed away. In the last hours, it is said that she asked Jefferson not to marry again. And he agreed, knowing Martha did not wish her children raised by a stepmother, as she had been.

Years later, Jefferson's daughter Patsy wrote, "He fainted, and remained so long insensible that they feared he never would revive. . . . He kept to his room three weeks, and . . . I was his constant companion — a solitary witness to many a burst of grief."

Later he rode horseback incessantly through the Albemarle woods and hills, with ten-year-old Patsy

*On September 6, Jefferson entered in his journal, "my dear wife died this day at 11:45 am."*

his silent partner. A special bond of love formed between them during this difficult time. Martha was buried near her children under the oak tree on the side of the mountain. Of the six children she had borne, only Patsy and Polly lived to adulthood.

No portrait exists of Thomas Jefferson's wife, and Jefferson destroyed his letters to her. In his *Autobiography* he wrote that he "lost the cherished companion of my life, in whose affections, unabated on both sides, I had lived the last ten years in unchequered happiness."

Jefferson's friends realized that he needed new interests. Through the efforts of delegate James

Madison, Jefferson's appointment was renewed as a member of the peace commission in Europe. The commission was negotiating the treaty with England after the Revolutionary War. Jefferson gladly accepted, but his travel could not be arranged right away. And before he could leave, the news came that John Adams and the American commissioners had already signed the peace treaty in Paris, so he did not make the trip.

In the year 1783, the master of Monticello spent time in his library cataloging and classifying his collection of 2640 books. Often he played games or taught school to Patsy, now eleven, and to Dabney Carr's six children. Jefferson also sent Madison his finished draft of the new constitution for Virginia, a plan that was very similar to the United States Constitution in its division of government and rights of the people.

In the fall the Congress of the Confederation elected Jefferson and he took his seat in Annapolis, Maryland, where they were now meeting. Before leaving, he arranged for Patsy to stay with Mrs. Thomas Hopkinson, mother of Francis Hopkinson, one of the signers of the Declaration of Independence. Jefferson worked out a rigorous schedule for her: "From 8 to 10, practice music. From 10 to 1, dance one day and draw another. From 1 to 2, draw on the day you dance and write a letter next day. From 3 to 4, read French. From 4 to 5, exercise yourself in music. From 5 to bedtime, read English, write, etc."

Jefferson also demanded a rigorous schedule of

himself. This was necessary because there were few delegates sent by each state. In this small congress he served on practically every committee and drafted thirty-one state papers in five months. Jefferson was disturbed when he found only seven delegates there to discuss the most important business, the treaty of peace. Finally, delegates from the two more states needed for ratification were rounded up, and the statement of ratification, prepared by Jefferson, was passed.

On September 3, 1783, the Treaty of Paris was signed, ending the Revolutionary War. Through the efforts of Benjamin Franklin, John Jay, and John Adams, the treaty gained independence for the thirteen colonies and possession of a great western domain that stretched to the Mississippi River.

One of the most important of Jefferson's committee reports was the "Ordinance of 1784." In it he outlined plans for the future government of the Northwest Territory, the region between the Ohio and Mississippi rivers and extending north around the Great Lakes. The new territories would be admitted to the Union on equal status with the thirteen original states. Ten new states would be formed, with republican governments, no hereditary titles allowed, and slavery not permitted after 1800. Jefferson's report became the basis for the Northwest Ordinance passed in 1787.

Jefferson's last report as congressman concerned the disorderly monetary system. He said, "Certainly, in all cases where we are free to choose between easy and difficult modes of operation, it is most rational to choose the easy." His "Notes on the Establishment of a Money Unit and a Coinage for the United States" established the dollar as the basic American currency. In 1786, Congress would enact the full plan of coinage he recommended, based on the decimal system.

In May 1784, Jefferson was named one of the commissioners who would negotiate commercial treaties with the European nations. At last he would visit Europe, joining commissioners Franklin and Adams in France. Proceeding quickly, he made arrangements for little Polly and Lucy Elizabeth to stay with Aunt Elizabeth and Uncle Francis Eppes at the Eppington plantation on the Appomattox River below Richmond. James Madison would direct the education of Peter and Dabney Carr, Jr., Jefferson's nephews, and the neighbors would supervise his farmlands.

Jefferson picked up Patsy, who would go with him, from Mrs. Hopkinson in Philadelphia. At four o'clock in the morning of July 5, they sailed from Boston for Paris via the Isle of Wight, England, and Le Havre, France, on the ship *Ceres*. Their 4600-mile trip took forty-one days, twenty-one of them by sea.

# 7
# *Minister to France*
# *1784–1790*

**U**pon arriving at his hotel in Paris, Jefferson sent for the tailor to measure him for a new outfit, and then purchased a new sword and belt, buckles, and lace ruffles. Before settling down to official business, he felt the Jeffersons should be dressed in the Parisian mode. Twelve-year-old Patsy wrote a friend, "We were obliged to send immediately for the stay [corset] maker, the mantua [gown] maker, the milliner and even a shoemaker before I could go out."

Jefferson enrolled his long-legged, redheaded daughter in the convent Abbaye Royal de Panthemont, where Patsy rapidly learned the language from the French girls. Although her father could read French fluently, he was still learning to speak the language.

At Benjamin Franklin's home in the nearby village of Passy, he, Adams, and Jefferson met for discussions. The American states wished to negotiate free trade with Europe and their possessions, especially in the West Indies. America's products — fish, tobacco, rice, lumber, and furs — needed markets. Since the revolution, respect for America had declined. The Old World governments in Europe did not believe in this weak republic across the sea.

Jefferson was not only interested in his diplomatic mission, he was also eager to learn more about the art, music, sculpture, and architecture of Europe. With the help of the popular Franklin, and the Marquis de Lafayette and his lovely wife Adrienne, Jefferson was introduced to French society. He attended balls, the theater, and musical concerts, and was frequently found visiting the shops and bookstalls.

Jefferson also charmed John Adams's wife, Abigail, known for her vivid and sometimes caustic letters about people. The Adams's oldest son, John Quincy, and their daughter Abigail were in France with them. They enjoyed Jefferson's company and Jefferson treated John Quincy like a son.

In January of 1785, Lafayette returned to France bringing back letters from America. In one of them to Jefferson, he read the crushing news that little Lucy Elizabeth, just two and a half years old, had died in an epidemic of whooping cough, along with the youngest Eppes child. That winter Jefferson suffered from migraine headaches but by March he was walking four or five miles a day

*Abigail Adams,
wife of John Adams.*

again. However, his depression and melancholy persisted. He was not happy in Paris and saw much of the French society as "empty bustle."

But there was much to admire in France. Besides the beautiful art and architecture, Jefferson wanted to see the countryside. And he raved about the food, such as the delicious French bread, the specially prepared peas, and potatoes, the wine, the sauces. Jefferson brought James Hemings, one of his most intelligent slaves, with him on the *Ceres,* and Hemings learned the art of Parisian cooking from some of the best chefs in Paris. As Jefferson's home was open to travelers, he needed his staff to be prepared for much entertaining.

Often Jefferson wrote his friends Madison and Monroe, asking them to join him for the summer, but they couldn't get away. Madison kept Jefferson informed of developments in America and Jefferson wrote back about France and sent along books. In one of his letters Jefferson was enthusiastic about the new French invention of "Phosphoretic matches." He wrote, "By having them [matches] at your bedside with a candle, the latter may be lighted at any moment of the night without getting out of bed."

Toward the end of April 1785, Congress appointed John Adams as America's first ambassador to England. About a week later Thomas Jefferson and Benjamin Franklin also received instructions. The elderly Franklin's request to return home because of poor health had been granted. Jefferson was appointed as the new ambassador to France, following in the footsteps of a great American statesman. When asked by one of Franklin's admirers if he had come to replace Franklin, Jefferson answered, "I am succeeding Franklin. No one can replace him."

At that time there was no consistent American policy for trade with Europe. Each state was free to adopt its own restrictions. Jefferson wrote John Jay in Philadelphia about the rude attitude of England and France toward the American ministers and their efforts to obtain treaties. He sent "Instructions" to help diplomats who would represent the United States abroad, and outlined future goals.

Because the Barbary pirates kept looting ships in the Mediterranean, Jefferson saw a need for an

American navy. The pirates had captured American ships and crews, holding them for ransom. In 1786, in London, Adams and Jefferson had negotiated but had failed to get the captives released. After Jefferson returned from France, Thomas Barclay succeeded in obtaining a peace treaty. Yet the Barbary pirates continued to plunder ships.

Back at the Virginia assembly, James Madison had won approval, without a single change, of Jefferson's bill for religious freedom. He wrote his friend the good news and mentioned that Congress had again selected him as minister to France for three more years.

Besides diplomatic letters, Jefferson had been writing to persuade Polly to come to France. He wanted her to leave during the summer months when it was safer to cross the ocean, and he wrote, "You will have as many dolls and playthings as you want," but she politely refused.

So one day, nine-year-old Polly was brought aboard ship, supposedly to play. Polly grew tired and fell asleep and, when she woke up, she was surprised to find they were out to sea. James Hemings' half-sister Sally, a fourteen-year-old mulatto slave, took care of her, and soon Polly became the darling of the crew.

Arriving in London, they stayed three weeks with Abigail Adams. Polly adored her and did not wish to leave. But finally the Jeffersons were reunited in Paris, and Polly and Patsy attended school together at the Abbye.

One of the guests whom Jefferson invited to

Paris was John Trumbull, a promising young artist. Trumbull planned to paint the events of the American Revolution. Today a replica of his best-known work, *The Signing of the Declaration of Independence*, hangs in the U.S. Capitol rotunda.

Among other artists that Jefferson met were the gentle, talented Maria Hadfield Cosway and her husband. Jefferson invited them to tour Paris with him. After a while it was only Maria and Thomas who visited the museums and had tea together. However, after a few months, Maria returned to London with her husband. Maria and Thomas continued their friendship with letters.

There is an account of Jefferson's walk one day in Paris with a lady. On this occasion, he decided to jump over a small fence and fell, dislocating his right wrist. After the incident, he wrote with his left hand for a month. Jefferson wrote, "How the right hand became disabled would be a long story for the left to tell. It was by one of those follies from which good cannot come, but ill may."

Was he trying to prove that American men were not inferior? In *Notes on Virginia*, Jefferson had refuted claims made by European naturalists that a degenerative process in America made men and animals smaller in size and vitality. As one proof, Jefferson had sent French scientist Buffon the skeleton of an American moose. Jefferson said that Buffon had "confounded," or confused, American moose with European reindeer. Years later Thomas Jefferson said that the reindeer was so small it could "walk under the Belly" of the moose.

The first edition of *Notes* was a small private printing in France meant only for a few friends and officials. A year earlier, Jefferson had sent an expanded copy, including a draft of the Virginia Constitution, to the secretary of the French Legion, Marbois.

Before Polly arrived, Jefferson had taken a four-month trip through the South of France. Along the way he asked questions of people he met, concerning the long hours they worked, the small amount of money they made, and the taxes they paid. A ragged woman told him she labored all day to earn eight sous, about eleven cents. Many were out of work. He urged Lafayette to make a trip incognito and wrote him, "You must ferret the people out of their hovels . . . look into their kettles, eat their bread."

While in France, Jefferson was asked to find an architect for the Virginia state capitol, and he appointed himself. He based his drawings on an ancient Roman temple, the Maison Carré in Nîmes, France. He had spent days seated before it, quietly observing its beauty.

Jefferson worked together with Charles-Louis Clérisseau preparing the designs, and in 1787 Jefferson sent the drawings to Virginia. The Virginia state capitol was the first building in America constructed in the form of a classical temple.

Jefferson's old friend William Short joined him his first winter in France as his private secretary. He brought with him a commission from Virginia for a statue to be constructed honoring George

Washington. Jefferson and Franklin searched for a fine sculptor and found Jean Antoine Houdon, one of the best on the Continent. Today, Houdon's statue of Washington stands in the capitol at Richmond.

During the busy year of 1787, the Congress adopted the Northwest Ordinance that established the government of the Northwest Territory. From May to September, a constitutional convention met, over which George Washington presided. Some delegates expected simply to amend the Articles of Confederation, which had proved to be a failure in governing the United States. The Articles gave Congress only limited powers to act on its decrees, meet obligations with other nations, or quell disorder. There were no federal courts or means of interstate trade. Instead, a new document was created. Madison, chief drafter of the Constitution, wrote to Jefferson about the fight to ratify it. The smaller states wished to retain their power and the larger states wanted the power to lie where there was population and wealth. But at last the disputes were settled. Jefferson liked the final document except that a bill of rights and the principle of limiting an electee's term of office were not included. However, the Bill of Rights was added within two years to guarantee individual liberties.

Madison's hard work earned him the title of "father of the Constitution." The document was signed on September 17, 1787, and ratified by the required number of nine states by June 21, 1788.

It was declared in effect on March 4, 1789. Also during that time, George Washington was chosen as the first president and John Adams as vice president.

In France, Jefferson heard the anger of the common people, discontented with their government's treatment of them. Lafayette tried to introduce a bill of rights for his own government, drawing on ideas from Jefferson's Declaration of Independence. But it was too late. On September 19, 1789, Jefferson wrote John Jay, "The patience of the people . . . has worn threadbare." The French Revolution had begun.

Jefferson had requested a leave to go home. So far, not much had been accomplished in the way of trade agreements by the American commissioners. Besides one treaty with Prussia in 1785, which had also been supported by Spain, attempts for treaties with Britain were unsuccessful. However, Jefferson had gained trade concessions from France, and a greater knowledge of European affairs. He had traveled in England, France, Italy, the Netherlands, and Germany. Along the way he had written in his notebooks and collected useful plants and animals to take back with him. After five years of service abroad, Jefferson and his two daughters sailed home on the *Clermont* in October.

After the Jefferson family arrived in Norfolk by carriage, they stopped at Richmond, Virginia, and visited the capitol under construction. Jefferson was surprised when people congratulated him as their new secretary of state. This was unwelcome news to him, since he had hoped to return to France.

Arriving at Monticello just before Christmas, the family, and especially Jefferson, was greeted with joy by the staff and slaves. Patsy later wrote, "When the door of the carriage opened, the negros received him in their arms and bore him to the house, crowding around . . . some blubbering and crying, others laughing."

The official letter from President Washington had been delivered notifying Jefferson of his appointment as secretary of state. Madison urged him to accept and said that his strong influence was needed against the pro-British supporters.

Also at the end of 1789, a welcome visitor, Thomas Mann Randolph, Jr., arrived at Monticello, returning after a four-year education in Edinburgh, Scotland. Patsy was delighted, as they

*Jefferson's daughter,*
*Martha (Patsy) Jefferson Randolph.*

had much in common and enjoyed talking together. Randolph knew a lot about farming, science, and politics. It wasn't too long before they were married.

After receiving a second letter from the President, Jefferson wrote Washington that he "no longer hesitated to undertake the office to which you are pleased to call me." With Polly staying at her Aunt Elizabeth's, forty-seven-year-old Jefferson left for his new career in New York City, the nation's temporary capital. As secretary of state, Jefferson's main goal was a foreign policy to strengthen America's commerce and take a neutral stand in European wars. In March, he presented himself to President George Washington and met the other Cabinet members: Alexander Hamilton, secretary of the treasury; Henry Knox, secretary of war; and Edmund Randolph, attorney general.

In a rented house on Maiden Lane, Jefferson tackled stacks of mail. There were requests from senators and representatives, besides odd matters to attend to that didn't fit into any other departments, such as Indian affairs, weights and measures, patents, and lighthouses. International relations came first. In a letter to Lafayette, Jefferson wrote, "I shall be sincere in my friendship to you and your nation."

But as he dined around town with others, Jefferson discovered there was a large and powerful group of Americans who favored Britain rather than France. The new treasury secretary, Alexander Hamilton, was the center of a group with

*Jefferson's political opponent Alexander Hamilton.*

those leanings. Young Colonel Hamilton, once Washington's aide during the war, commanded attention and Washington respected his opinions. The Federalists, as Hamilton's supporters came to be called, urged that the Cabinet agree to Hamilton's recommendations for financing the country. Hamilton, with John Jay and James Madison, had written *The Federalist Papers*, which had swung votes in favor of the Constitution. Now Hamilton's policies succeeded in putting the government's finances in order. He restored credit abroad through his plan to repay the enormous Revolutionary War debt.

At Cabinet meetings, Hamilton presented quite a splash dressed in silk and lace finery, in contrast to Jefferson's simple clothes. The contrast was not

93

only in how the two men dressed but in their political ideals as well. While Hamilton favored close ties with England, Jefferson preferred to strengthen the old attachment to France. Hamilton wanted a strong central government with power in the hands of the bankers, manufacturers, and holders of large estates. Jefferson believed in a strict interpretation of the Constitution to limit the powers of central government. And he believed in a rural economy and independence achieved by farming the land.

In New York, in the spring of 1790, Jefferson had another attack of migraine for two months. He wrote his daughters saying how much he missed them. Was Patsy pleasing her husband? Did Polly know how to sew a hem? Patsy replied with the good news that she and Tom were moving to a farm closer to Monticello, and that love for her husband and his needs came first in her life "except my love for you."

In the House of Representatives, Madison had backed Hamilton's first bill to repay the federal debt. But in the spring of 1790, Madison and Jefferson argued against Hamilton's second bill, which would allow the government to absorb the war debt of all states. This would mean that the government would pay face value to people holding Continental dollars and bills of credit, which was higher than their market value.

Madison objected because wealthy speculators had rushed in to buy up the bonds and paper debts at low prices and would collect large profits. Some

My dear Maria       New York June 13. 1790.    1000

I have recieved your letter of May 23. which was in answer
to mine of May 2. but I wrote you also on the 23d. of May, so that
you still owe me an answer to that, which I hope is now on the road.
in matters of correspondence as well as of money you must never be
in debt. I am much pleased with the account you give me of your
occupations, and the making the pudding is as good an article of them
as any. when I come to Virginia I shall insist on eating a pudding
of your own making, as well as on trying other specimens of your
skill. you must make the most of your time while you are with
so good an aunt who can learn you every thing. we had not
peas nor strawberries here till the 8th. day of this month. on the
same day I heard the first Whip-poor-will whistle. swallows and
martins appeared here on the 21st. of April. when did they appear with
you? and when had you peas, strawberries, & whip-poor-wills in
Virginia? take notice hereafter whether the whip-poor-wills always
come with the strawberries & peas. send me a copy of the maxims
I gave you, also a list of the books I promised you. A friend
had a long touch of my periodical head-ach, but a very moderate
one. it has not quite left me yet. Adieu, my dear, love your
aunt & cousins, and me more than all.
           Your's affectionately,
           Th: Jefferson.

Miss Maria Jefferson.

*A letter from Jefferson to his daughter Maria (Polly), June 13, 1790.*

states had already paid their war debts and some had not. Hamilton was losing to persuasive Madison, so he turned to Jefferson and asked for help to get the so-called Assumption bill passed.

Jefferson felt he was a "stranger to the subject" but did not wish to see the young republic torn apart. To promote an understanding, Jefferson invited Hamilton and Madison to dinner with two other members of the Virginia delegation.

Madison wanted to work out a compromise. At that time, there was much discussion about where to locate the national capital. The southerners wanted the capital city to be situated on the Potomac River. So Hamilton offered a trade. If Madison and the southerners would vote for his Assumption bill, Hamilton would swing his supporters to vote for the Potomac location.

At last the lawmakers reached an agreement and passed the Assumption bill. The capital was moved from New York City to Philadelphia and, during 1791 and 1792, President Washington chose the precise location on the Potomac that is now Washington, D.C. He asked Jefferson to draw plans, define the boundaries, and interpret the federal law. The French engineer, Major Pierre L'Enfant, designed the buildings along the lines of Jefferson's classical style and the new "federal city" was built over a period of ten years.

# 8
# Secretary of State
# 1790–1796

After the Assumption bill compromise, Jefferson and Hamilton's difference of opinion deepened. Hamilton was ambitious and dreamed of an aristocracy of wealth to control the country. He would deliberately misinterpret to England Jefferson's intentions when Jefferson's policy did not agree with his own. In one instance, Jefferson's important state paper to Britain on the surrender of western forts was blandly ignored by Britain's ambassador, George Hammond, because Hamilton had said that President Washington had not approved it.

In 1791 Hamilton moved to establish the Bank of the United States, which would be half public, half private. Madison opposed him, and Washington questioned if the bill would be unconstitutional. Jefferson said any disputed clause in the

Constitution must be *strictly interpreted* by the Tenth Amendment. This amendment reserved for the states and the people all powers not specifically delegated to the federal government. In defense of his bill, Hamilton wrote that the Constitution had "implied powers" granted to the federal government. This argument convinced Washington and he signed the bank bill into law.

After a year in office, Jefferson suspected Hamilton's intrigue. Hamilton was building a political party machine, and Jefferson and Madison decided they should play the same political game. The two went on a vacation for a month, and visited New York, where they talked to some influential people who disliked Hamilton's rough tactics. They met Colonel Aaron Burr, a brilliant attorney. He told them about the Sons of Saint Tammany who favored voting for the Republicans, those who shared Jefferson's political ideas. This party, also called the Democratic-Republican party, would later become the Democratic party.

Before returning to Philadelphia, Jefferson and Madison also talked to poet Philip Freneau about starting a newspaper dedicated to Republican principles. It was not until 1791 that Freneau's *National Gazette* appeared in Philadelphia. It was strongly Republican, influenced by Jefferson's supporters.

Two years earlier, in New York City, John Fenno, the editor of the weekly *Gazette of the United States,* a very influential newspaper for Hamilton and the Federalist cause, had published a series of "discourses" by John Adams that seemed to support a reign of monarchs and noblemen.

Then Fenno had published remarks by Jefferson in the newspaper. Jefferson's remarks referred to Tom Paine's *Rights of Man* and stated that he was glad that something was being said against "the political heresies that have sprung up among us."

When Adams read Jefferson's remarks, he took them as a personal attack. Articles attacking Paine and Jefferson appeared in the newspapers, with words flying back and forth from angry supporters replying to the charges.

Jefferson did not like the hard feelings and wrote Adams, "That you and I differ in our ideas as to the best form of government is well known to us both . . . but we have differed as friends shall do, respecting the purity of each other's motives and confining our differences of opinion to private conversation." Adams replied, "The friendship that has subsisted for fifteen years between us . . . is very dear to my heart."

On July 4, 1791, the first Bank of the United States opened. Alexander Hamilton promoted the idea, hoping to finance more manufacturing and business enterprises. Madison predicted that the rich would get richer and the farmer would not benefit at all. Rumors of a dividend of twelve percent, a very high return for money invested, brought a wild rush of speculators eager to buy stock. This crippled the bank, the bank ran out of funds, and the Treasury Department had to rescue it. The following year the same thing happened.

After the bank fiasco, Jefferson hoped the Hamiltonian reign was over. But in spite of his failures, the wealthy aristocracy continued to support Hamilton.

Jefferson was lonely without his family, and sent for Polly, enrolling her in an academy run by a Mrs. Pine. Aunt Elizabeth Eppes's son Jack came to study under Jefferson's supervision. Jefferson was glad to see him and to return some of the loving care that Jack's mother had given Polly for many years. At age thirteen, Polly had grown beautiful and, since her visit to France, she liked to be called Maria. Jack, her cousin, noticed the change in her from childhood days.

Jefferson lived on Market Street, three blocks from Washington's presidential mansion. As he continued to entertain guests, he thought of his butler in Paris and sent for him to run his household. In Virginia, Patrick Henry heard of the wonderful dinners at Jefferson's house, where people were eating strange new desserts, including *ice cream*.

Hamilton was still attacking Jefferson. In his newspaper he wrote, under the signature "An American," that Jefferson had paid Freneau to publish a newspaper that undermined not only the government but the Constitution. Immediately, Freneau and others replied to this lie, and an angry Hamilton wrote back under the alias "Scourge." Much displeased, Washington asked Jefferson and

Hamilton to explain their problem. In his letter to President Washington, Jefferson wrote, "No government ought to be without censure; and where the press is free, no one ever will."

On his return to Philadelphia from Monticello, Jefferson stopped to see Washington at Mount Vernon. He wanted to make sure the President remembered that Jefferson wanted to retire in six months, at the end of Washington's first term. Washington told him he was undecided about his own retirement. Jefferson reminded him how much he was needed: "The confidence of the whole union is centered on you." Washington replied that if he continued in office, Jefferson should also.

Jefferson sent a letter to his sister Martha at Monticello that he would be detained for the summer; Washington had decided to serve as president again. Two months later England and France went to war. The Americans were on the side of their old allies, the French people, who fought not only the British but also the Austrian and Prussian soldiers supporting King Louis XVI.

Jefferson wrote Washington telling him that war had broken out, but the letter did not reach him. In it he advised him to honor America's treaty with France, signed in 1778. Jefferson wished to try a tactic of playing off the two enemies, France and England, to the advantage of America.

But Hamilton had already prevented this strategy by assuring British Ambassador Hammond that America would stay neutral. At the Cabinet meeting on April 19, 1793, President Washington had already received a list of requests sympathetic to Britain from Hamilton. The secretary of the Treasury asked for a declaration of neutrality. Jefferson argued that if Britain and France were forced to bid for neutrality, Congress could ask a price in exchange. But Hamilton said that remaining silent was dangerous, since it could be interpreted that America was siding with France. They finally agreed on a proclamation without the word "neutrality."

Jefferson had previously instructed Gouverneur Morris, ambassador to France, to recognize the new French government. Now the question was whether to receive their Ambassador Genêt. If Congress denied him, it placed America on the side of kings. Hamilton disagreed, saying the treaty was void between the two nations because of the change in government. But Jefferson argued that beyond question the treaty was valid. President Washington decided to receive Genêt.

Ambassador Genêt was both arrogant and quarrelsome. He demanded repayment of all debt to France — $2,500,000 — although only one-fifth was due in 1793. Secretary of the Treasury Hamilton refused. Genêt even commissioned American privateers to raid English ships. Secretary of State Jefferson wrote him that the President wanted no more privateers commissioned in U.S. ports.

Genêt wrote back that he would defer to the President's wishes, but he then took *Little Sarah*, a captured British brigantine, mounted fourteen cannon on her, and sent her to sea. Hamilton was furious and demanded that Genêt be publicly embarrassed and recalled to France.

Jefferson with his quiet wisdom said, "Friendly nations negotiate their difference in private. . . . If Genêt's letters were forwarded to France they would quietly recall him." Then Jefferson sat down and wrote one of his most diplomatic letters, which contained "many expressions of affection" for the cause of France, regardless of their Ambassador Genêt's conduct.

By this time the American people did not like President Washington's stand on neutrality and he was ridiculed in the newspapers. Jefferson had returned to Monticello, and Washington came to him and asked him not to retire. He was needed not only for himself but also as the Republican voice on a Cabinet of Federalists. Jefferson agreed to serve six more months.

In 1793, Jefferson resigned, with letters to Washington expressing goodwill between them. As secretary of state, Jefferson had achieved an outstanding record. His foreign policy was tolerant and open-minded, based on the interests of the individual as opposed to Hamilton's belief in a strong central government controlled by a wealthy aristocracy.

In 1794, Jefferson said good-bye to Madison and Monroe, both members of the new Congress. He knew Madison would defend the Republican position. All the way home, Jefferson rejoiced to be returning to Monticello. He had missed his family, his sister Martha, and his grandchildren. Anne and

Thomas J. Randolph were waiting for him to play with them.

But there was also much for Jefferson to do on his farm property of 10,647 acres, 2000 of them under cultivation. During his career of public service, the land had been left in the hands of overseers who had farmed out the soil. In 1793–1794 Jefferson used a program of crop rotation to restore the land, planted grain, and looked for other means of income until his farm would be productive again.

Jefferson had invented a moldboard of least resistance that made plowing the farm easier. Sketched out in 1788, it was the curved part behind the plowshare (the metal bladelike part) and needed less force to pull it than other plows. Jefferson said that he "never thought of monopolizing by patent any useful idea which happened to offer itself to me."

Jefferson also wrote directions for what he called a "cipher wheel," which he probably used to decode and encode messages while he was secretary of state. The device was made of removable wooden disks, with letters of the alphabet imprinted on their outer edges. For his correspondence, Jefferson used his "polygraph," a letter-copying device with two pens, which he called "the finest invention of the present age."

Now that Jefferson was home, he struggled with the mounting interest due on debts he had accumulated. The farm was necessary to provide income, but with land opening in the West, it was

*Jefferson's polygraph. When he wrote with one pen, the other followed as his hand moved.*

difficult to obtain workers. As one solution, Jefferson sent for the Virginian Hugh Petit to superintend the work at Monticello.

To raise money, Jefferson went into business. He started training his slave boys to make nails. The nailers got special food, clothing, and rations; the managers received cash bonuses. He discouraged any overseer from whipping a worker, and chose a black man to be the nailery boss. The men produced a ton and a half of nails each month to sell to retailers and farmers. Also Jefferson used many of the nails in remodeling his house.

It was three years of busy, sometimes happy times for Jefferson at Monticello. He had time for his gardens and sketched plans for terraces of fruit trees, strawberry beds, and a vineyard. His slave Isaac recalled his master as a "straight-up man" who was heard "singing when riding or walking."

But politics did not leave him alone. Madison, as well as many other Republican leaders, wrote him the news several times a week. He read about the Whiskey Rebellion in western Pennsylvania, an uprising by Scotch-Irish farmers against a federal excise tax. Secretary of the Treasury Hamilton had imposed the tax on whiskey, and militiamen had been sent to suppress the settler's rebellion.

*A 1845 daguerreotype of Isaac, one of Jefferson's slaves.*

Jefferson heard about England's restricting American trade and seizing American ships and sailors. Washington had sent Chief Justice Jay as special envoy to England to settle their differences. In 1795, Jay at last worked out a treaty that provided for the evacuation of western forts and relaxed trade barriers, but did not concede the United States much else.

It had become clear to Madison that the Republican cause was not succeeding and that Jefferson was needed to run for president. Jefferson was asked to leave Monticello and lead the Republican party to victory in the election of 1796. President Washington had refused another term and Madison had become a one-party figure because of his battles with Hamilton. He had just married Dolley Payne Todd and wished to retire.

Jefferson wondered if he was prepared for this political battle. John Adams was the Federalists' candidate for president. But Hamilton was scheming to throw the election to Thomas Pinckney of South Carolina, the Federalists' vice presidential candidate. Jefferson decided he should run for the Republicans.

The system of election in the Constitution called for the legislature of each state to choose a given number of electors, each of whom had two votes. Jefferson would not choose his running mate. As yet, political parties were not set up to lobby for the candidates. It was believed that the electors would choose the two best men available. The man with the most votes would be president and the runner-up his vice president.

Hamilton asked the Federalists in South Carolina, Pinckney's home state, to throw away their votes for Adams and to cast just one vote for Pinckney. He was assuming that the Federalists in other states would vote for both candidates and Pinckney would come out ahead with eight votes. Pinckney would become president and indebted to Hamilton.

But the news leaked out and Jefferson's vice presidential candidate, Aaron Burr, the ambitious New York politician, warned New England electors of Hamilton's plot. The electors threw away enough second votes to elect their favorite son, John Adams. Strangely enough, three Republicans changed their vote to Adams at the last minute and he was elected president by three votes. Jefferson placed second and became vice president.

Two men of different political beliefs, Jefferson the Republican, and Adams the Federalist, had been elected to work together. This might become an awkward situation. However, Jefferson believed that his only duty was to preside over the Senate and make sure that it performed its duties within the limits of the Constitution. And he hoped to spend more time at home.

# 9
# *Vice President to President 1797–1805*

In late February of 1797 Jefferson packed his law and history books and traveled to Philadelphia to accept the office of vice president of the United States. He also had been elected president of the American Philosophical Society, a group established for the promotion of useful knowledge.

The society had asked Jefferson for a copy of his book *Notes on Virginia*. In it, Jefferson had described his findings at an Indian burial mound near Charlottesville. His theory of interpreting soil layers proved to be one of the basic principles used by archaeologists today.

In Philadelphia the vice president planned to enjoy the "philosophical evenings in the winter, and rural days in the summer." That same year, Jefferson's second daughter, Maria (formerly

Polly), was married to John Wayles Eppes in a lovely fall ceremony at Monticello.

During his vice presidency, Jefferson would support President Adams as much as possible. Although political enemies, they were also friends. But there was a social wall and sometimes bitter feelings between party members. Each day, Jefferson dined with officials who supported his belief in commercial treaties abroad and opposed the Federalists' arguments in favor of isolation. However, as vice president, Jefferson had no power to make changes.

The Republicans had a slight lead in the House of Representatives, while the Federalists held a majority of more than two to one in the Senate. With the threat of a possible war with France

*President John Adams, from a portrait by John Singleton Copley.*

hanging over their heads, the Federalists passed three unpopular laws known as the Alien and Sedition Acts.

Jefferson considered these laws a direct challenge to individual liberty. Two of them gave the president power to expel or imprison aliens; one of them made naturalization more difficult; another, the Sedition Act, punished those who wrote or spoke "with intent to defame" the government. Although the acts were not strictly enforced, the editors of several Jeffersonian newspapers were convicted under the Sedition Act.

In protest, Jefferson and Madison drafted the Kentucky and Virginia Resolutions in 1798 and 1799. The resolutions said that the states could declare unconstitutional any powers or acts of the government not authorized by the Constitution under the Bill of Rights. As vice president, Jefferson's connection with the resolutions was kept secret.

For his Senate duties, Jefferson wrote the *Manual of Parliamentary Practice for the Use of the Senate of the United States*. The guide was based on his background of law studies with George Wythe, and his court experiences. The manual has been translated into several languages and is still read today.

By the time of the presidential election of 1800, the Federalists had almost destroyed themselves in the eyes of the voting public with their unpopular laws. Still, it looked like the Federalists might win the election. Jefferson was persuaded to run

# REPUBLICANS

## Turn out, turn out and save your Country from ruin !

From an *Emperor*—from a *King*—from the iron grasp of a *British Tory Faction*—an unprincipled banditti of British speculators. The hireling tools and emissaries of his majesty king George the 3d have thronged our city and diffused the poison of principles among us.

### DOWN WITH THE TORIES, DOWN WITH THE BRITISH FACTION,

Before they have it in their power to enslave you, and reduce your families to distress by heavy taxation. Republicans want no Tribute-liars—they want no ship Ocean-liars—they want no Rufus King's for Lords —they want no Varick to lord it over them—they want no Jones for senator, who fought with the British against the Americans in time of the war.—But they want in their places such men as

### *Jefferson & Clinton,*

who fought their Country's Battles in the year '76

*A political campaign broadside from the election of 1800.*

again for president as a Democratic-Republican with Aaron Burr as the vice presidential candidate. John Adams was the Federalist candidate for president, with Charles Cotesworth Pinckney as vice president.

In a close election, the result was a tie in electoral votes between Jefferson and Burr. Under the existing laws, Congress had to decide between the two men. Jefferson was privately asked to make certain promises to the Federalists and was told that if he did so, his election would be assured. But Jefferson refused to compromise his principles.

112

Then, by a strange twist of fate, Hamilton, who had opposed Jefferson so many times, changed his mind about Burr and wrote to his constituents, "Jefferson is to be preferred. He is by far not so dangerous a man; and he has pretentions to character." After weeks of balloting thirty-six times, Jefferson was named president, with Aaron Burr, the second highest vote-getter, vice president.

Commenting on his election, Jefferson called it a second American Revolution, "as real a revolution in the principles of government as that of 1776 was in form." Thus began the Jeffersonian years of government.

On the first Wednesday in March 1801, the new President of the United States walked the two blocks from his hotel to the partially completed Capitol. This tall, redheaded gentleman was accompanied by members of Congress on each side of him. Jefferson was almost fifty-eight years old, the third president of the nearly twenty-five-year-old republic.

That morning the company of Washington artillery and the Alexandria riflemen paraded in front of Jefferson's hotel. As he entered the Senate chamber, the militia fired their guns. Jefferson looked out at the crowded room; John Adams and other Federalists were conspicuously absent.

In Jefferson's eloquent speech, he called on his fellow citizens to "unite with one heart and mind" and declared, "Every difference of opinion is not a difference in principle. . . . We are all Republicans — we are all Federalists." He went on to clearly state the principles of democratic government.

Jefferson chose not to make any drastic changes in the "midnight" judgeships appointed by Adams at the last minute before he left office. Congress quickly approved Jefferson's Cabinet: Virginian James Madison for the State Department; Massachusetts Republicans Levi Lincoln for attorney general, and Henry Dearborn, secretary of war; Pennsylvanian Albert Gallatin as secretary of the treasury. Robert Smith of Baltimore consented to be secretary of the navy. These were the men with whom Jefferson would share his decisions.

In April, Jefferson moved into the vacant President's House in Washington, ready to go to work. In May he read reports that Tripoli pirates had raided U.S. ships in the Mediterranean. The angry Algerians had asked for their bribe money, promised during the Adams administration, and the *pasha* of Tripoli had declared war on the United States.

Unlike Washington and Adams, Jefferson consulted closely with his Cabinet. The unscrupulous rulers of Algiers, Tunis, and Tripoli had long preyed upon Mediterranean commerce. The only ships spared were those whose country paid the pirates an annual tribute.

Jefferson was determined to end the system of bribes by a show of force. He sent the overdue payment along with a naval unit to guard America's ships. Between 1802 and 1805, gunboats successfully challenged the Barbary pirates, and diplomats at last secured a treaty providing for "peace without tribute."

On New Year's Day of 1802, a clergyman from Massachusetts brought President Jefferson a tribute of a different kind: an enormous cheese which his town had produced. President Jefferson thanked the clergyman and said that he liked the cheese but couldn't accept it as a gift. He insisted on paying the town 200 dollars, which they gratefully accepted.

Unlike that of his predecessors, Jefferson's policy was frugal. In Congress he repealed the taxes that were difficult to collect, such as the whiskey tax. Except for the Tripolian War, Treasury Secretary Gallatin reduced the national debt almost three million dollars a year. Jefferson cut the cost of the army, the navy, and the diplomatic service abroad. With America at peace, more money came in from customs receipts on goods traded with the mainland of Europe.

Jefferson repealed the Federalist Judiciary Act, which had expanded the expensive court program, and passed a new judiciary act. He let the Alien and Sedition Acts expire and pardoned all those who had been jailed under these laws. In July, one of those pardoned, James Callender, visited Jefferson in Washington asking to be appointed postmaster of Richmond. When Jefferson refused, the editor turned on him by printing malicious stories about Jefferson in his newspaper.

The President did not reply to these rumors from Callender and other editors, nor did he imprison them for libel. He felt it was ungentlemanly to reply, and he reaffirmed his belief in the freedom of the press. Callender wrote about Jefferson's assault on the "virtue of a lady," Betsy Walker, whom he had known in bachelor days. The "assault" was Jefferson's offer of love to Betsy. His love had been promptly refused, for the lady was married. He told friends that the rumor was the only one founded in truth, among all the allegations against him.

As the slanderous stories continued, Jefferson felt someone should stop the lies, and he asked for action at the state level. Republicans in Pennsylvania and New York indicted two of the editors. The indictment brought Hamilton out of retirement to defend them. But all of Hamilton's oratory did not persuade the New York legislature to release the editors, because the attack was on the President himself, not on a principle of the existing federal government. This case led to a new libel law that made *truth* the deciding element. Other states followed with laws that continue to protect newspapers from libel suits today.

In late November, Jefferson welcomed his two daughters who came to visit him in Washington. Martha and Maria had been busy with their families and could not get away sooner. It was a happy time for the Jeffersons, spending Christmas and New Year's together.

But Jefferson could not forget about foreign affairs. Although Europe was briefly at peace, the President had heard that Spain, now dominated

*A portrait of Thomas Jefferson painted by Mather Brown.*

by France, had secretly returned its Louisiana territory to the French. Jefferson had written the American ambassador to France, Robert Livingston, requesting that he persuade France to part with Louisiana, but there had been no answer. Ambitious Napoleon Bonaparte favored the scheme of his foreign minister, Talleyrand — to create a new French empire in the New World. Meanwhile, Spain had ordered the port in New Orleans to be closed. This act violated the treaty establishing commercial relations with Spain, negotiated by Envoy Extraordinary Thomas Pinckney in 1795.

Under the terms of the Treaty of San Lorenzo (Pinckney's treaty), Americans were granted the privilege of tax-free deposit, or temporary storage of goods, at New Orleans. The entire Mississippi River was open to navigation through Spanish territory. It also fixed boundaries of the United States with Louisiana and East and West Florida.

Napoleon was ambitious to expand his empire in the New World and had supported Spain's restriction of American settlers to the region east of the Alleghenies. But the population was increasing on both sides of the Ohio River and the people needed to transport and sell goods down the Mississippi, and out the Gulf of Mexico to places as far away as Europe. The colonists cried for war with France.

By 1803, with still no word from Livingston, President Jefferson sent Monroe as a special emissary to France to assist with negotiations. If a settlement over the Mississippi could not be reached, he planned to play one nation against the other. The United States would ask the British to help them expel the French from Louisiana.

By this time, the European scene had changed. Napoleon now needed money to finance a war with England, and he could get this money by selling the Louisiana land. Monroe arrived just as Livingston was in the final stages of purchasing New Orleans and other parts of the Louisiana province from the French.

In Congress, statesmen questioned whether the purchase was constitutional and thought an amendment was needed. Jefferson felt the opportunity was too good to pass up and believed he was justified in overlooking the Constitution in this case. He knew public support was behind him.

After weeks of bargaining, the French Minister Talleyrand suddenly asked: "What will you give for the whole?" Surprised, the envoys made offers until Talleyrand agreed. France signed a treaty April 30, 1803, to sell the Louisiana territory to America for about fifteen million dollars, or *less than three cents an acre.* In what came to be known as the Louisiana Purchase, Jefferson had acquired some 828,000 square miles, double the area of what was then the United States.

A few months after his inauguration, Jefferson had said to Monroe, "However our present interests may restrain us within our limits, it is impossible not to look forward to distant times when our rapid multiplication will expand it beyond those limits, and cover the whole northern if not the southern continent."

In June, Jefferson asked Congress for 2500 dollars to explore the vast wilderness area up the Missouri River, across the Great Divide, and into the valley of the Columbia River. The President appointed his secretary, Meriwether Lewis, and William Clark to lead an expedition of ten or twelve men.

At an early session in October 1803, Congress ratified the treaty with France. Money was needed for the purchase, and details had to be worked out for dividing the territory. Jefferson urged Congress to remain neutral during Napoleon's war with England.

Jefferson declared, "We should be most unwise indeed, were we to cast away the singular blessings of the position in which nature has placed us, the opportunity she has endowed us with of pursuing at a distance from foreign contentions, the paths of industry, peace, and happiness."

Along with Jefferson's habits of thrift, he liked a simple life. The White House was open to visitors every morning instead of having the formal afternoon parties as in the past. Jefferson said that since "4th of Mar. 1801 there is no [royal] court of the U.S." His informality was sometimes embarrassing to the ambassadors and envoys sent to talk to him. Early one morning Jefferson met an ambassador at the door, casually dressed, wearing slippers.

In November the new British minister, Anthony Merry, was invited to a dinner party that Jefferson gave for his Cabinet members and officials of the diplomatic corps and their wives. The Merrys expected it to be in their honor and a formal affair. Jefferson gave his arm to Dolley Madison, his unofficial hostess, and escorted her into the dining room first. Anthony Merry was upset to find himself seated facing the French ambassador, with whose country England was at war, and his wife seated in a less favorable location than the Spanish ambassador. The Merrys were offended and refused to visit the White House again.

The diplomat reported the incident to his government and Jefferson told Monroe, U.S. minister to England, about this minor crisis: "We have told him that the principle of society, as well as of government, with us, is the equality of the individuals composing it. That no man here would come to a dinner, where he was to be marked with inferiority to any other."

The President carried on lively conversation with his guests, but he also listened. His broad knowledge covered many scholarly topics, from chemistry and zoology to fine wines. One time when his daughter Martha (Patsy) proposed a toast to a fellow Virginian, her father gently reminded her that she was breaking one of his three laws at the table: "No healths, no politics, and no restraint." He wished people to be at their ease and have a pleasant time. There were no big parties, only galas on the Fourth of July and New Year's Day. Jefferson used his own money to entertain, one year spending nearly a third of his salary.

Often, Jefferson was not recognized in public places as the president. A story is told that one afternoon, as usual, Jefferson was riding about the outskirts of the little village of Washington. A Connecticut man noticed his fine horse, Wildair, and asked him for a "horse trade." Jefferson was not interested, but as they rode along, the men discussed politics. The Yankee declared that the President was a wasteful man who spent the citizens' hard-earned money; and besides that, he dressed in clothes and jewelry worth a fortune. Jefferson assured the New England gentleman that the President dressed about the same as himself.

As they were riding close to the White House, Jefferson suggested that they seek out the President. When a servant addressed Jefferson as "Mr. President," his startled new friend departed hastily.

At Monticello, Jefferson's youngest daughter, Maria, was about to give birth to a child. When the President learned that she was dangerously ill, he hurried home to be with her. Eight days later, on April 17, 1804, his beloved Maria, who looked so much like her mother, died at the age of twenty-five. In June he wrote his friend John Page, "Others may lose of their abundance; but, I, of my want, have lost even the half of all I had."

Toward the end of his term as vice president, Aaron Burr's friends in the New York legislature nominated him for the governorship. But Hamilton again used his influence and defeated Burr's bid for governor of New York.

Hatred had grown between the two men and, in July of 1804, Aaron Burr challenged Alexander Hamilton to a duel. In the duel, Hamilton was fatally wounded. The young republic had lost a strong leader, a statesman who had served his country well. President Jefferson had lost a powerful opponent. Although Burr was indicted for murder, the charges were dismissed and Burr returned to finish his term as vice president.

Jefferson accepted the offer to run for president again and in 1804 he was reelected by all of the sixteen states except Connecticut and Delaware. The remarkable vote in the electoral college was 162 to 14. By repeal of the Federalist Judiciary Act, he had gradually removed the Adams appointments and filled the vacancies with a number of Republican judgeships. The Seventh Congress had been cooperative and, by the opening of the Eighth Congress, the Republicans were in charge.

Jefferson was elated with the support for his presidency. His first administration had been marked by careful spending and a nation at peace. Jefferson hoped his second term would be as successful.

# 10
# The Second Presidency and the Tranquil Years 1805–1826

In 1805 Thomas Jefferson began a second term that would be marked with political intrigue and opposition. Yet he kept his party, the Congress, and the nation together. On this inaugural day, Jefferson led the parade to the U.S. Capitol mounted on his favorite horse, Wildair. In his speech Jefferson asked that surplus revenues in the national treasury be used for education, improvement of roads, and defense in wartime.

The year before, the Napoleonic Wars had begun in Europe and Jefferson realized that the United States must protect its neutral status and trade. The President believed in preparing only for defense. He would not endorse a provisional army and a seagoing navy as Alexander Hamilton and other members of Congress had suggested. However, Jefferson outlined two ways to protect the harbors of coastal towns: a trained militia that could move heavy cannon mounted on traveling carriages to any point, as needed; and other heavy cannon mounted on floating batteries and boats to stop vessels entering or leaving the harbors. In addition, 240 gunboats, at a cost of one million dollars, would be built over a period of ten years.

Jefferson again tried to bring pressure on Spain to sell the Florida Territories, and he urged Congress to buy the province. Both Republicans and Federalists opposed the idea, known as the "two million dollar purchase." Congress did finally approve the sale in 1806, but Spain, practically controlled by France, refused to be swayed by money, and Jefferson's plan failed. Years after Jefferson left office, Florida would become part of the United States.

Meanwhile, it was rumored that ambitious Aaron Burr was involved in a conspiracy to separate the western states from the Union and become president of an independent government carved from the new Louisiana Territory. When Jefferson learned of the plot, Burr was seized and brought to trial as a traitor, charged with attempting secession of United States lands. The Federalist Chief Justice of the Supreme Court, John Marshall, Jefferson's opponent, did not convict him.

At Monticello the Randolph children, especially Ellen, were all excited about going to Washington.

They would spend the winter of 1805–1806 with "Grand Papa," as they called Jefferson. He had written Ellen that the executive mansion was a "great stone house, big enough for two emperors, one pope and the grand lama in the bargain."

Squeezed into a big carryall with four horses, the family left for Washington, 120 miles away. It was a long, hard trip and Martha was expecting a baby. They arrived safely, and soon a baby's cry was heard in the president's house, the first baby born there. Jefferson was so happy he promptly named him James Madison Randolph, after his friend.

That June, some sad, distressing news reached Jefferson. His old mentor and friend George Wythe had died a painful death from poison. It was believed that his nephew had killed him, as well as some servants remembered in the will, in order to inherit Wythe's estate.

In September, happier news came that the Lewis and Clark expedition had arrived in St. Louis. People had thought the men were dead. In more than two years the explorers had journeyed over 7000 miles. Lewis wrote Jefferson that he was certain he had "discovered the most practical route which does exist across the country."

Everyone was jubilant at their safe arrival, especially Jefferson. On their trip, Lewis and Clark had discovered 122 types of animals and 178 types of plants new to science, and they brought back information about the Indian tribes living in the West.

By December 1806, Lewis and Clark made it back to Washington. One of the Indian chiefs, Big White from the Mandan tribe, and his wife, had returned with them, and the chief was welcomed as a celebrity. The explorers were rewarded with land, pay raises, and military appointments.

Lewis and Clark brought Jefferson many American Indian artifacts, as well as plants for his garden. The large entrance hall to Jefferson's house was his museum. Antlers of the American moose and elk, and buffalo heads, were mounted on the north wall along with a large display of Indian objects. The south wall held his collection of natural history objects, which included mastodon bones and tusks from William Clark's dig in Kentucky.

Jefferson turned his attention back to world affairs. The war between Great Britain and France had damaged America's economy. Many U.S. ships, attempting to trade with foreign nations, had been seized and both sailors and cargo abducted by France and Britain. In the spring of 1807, Jefferson called for the Embargo Act, which he called a policy of "peaceful coercion," to cool the pro-war demands at home.

The Embargo Act, in effect from 1807 to 1809, forbade all international trade to and from American ports. It was Jefferson's attempt to convince

*A political cartoon depicting Jefferson, being robbed by both King George III of Great Britain and Napoleon of France.*

the warring nations to respect America's rights to neutral commerce. But the act failed because it was too difficult to enforce. Britain suffered little and France had already lost most of her trade with America before the Embargo Act.

There were bitter protests against Jefferson's Democratic-Republican policies, and open talk of secession. The embargo had shut down ports, decreased the exports of cotton and tobacco, and greatly reduced agriculture in the South. Across the sea, U.S. ministers James Monroe and William Pinkney had failed to obtain a satisfactory treaty with Great Britain.

Jefferson wrote Secretary of the Treasury Gallatin, "The Embargo law is certainly the most embarrassing one we have ever had to execute."

On New Year's Day, 1808, a law went into effect prohibiting the importation of slaves from Africa. Jefferson was glad to see this happen. In his *Notes on Virginia* he had favored some sort of gradual emancipation. However, the law did not stop slavery altogether, and it increased hard feelings between the anti-slavery North and the slave-dependent South.

Jefferson had refused to run again when asked, so in January of 1808 the Republican congressional caucus nominated James Madison for president and George Clinton for vice president. James Monroe had also been nominated and Jefferson wrote him, hoping he would support Madison so that the party would not split their vote. Although Monroe did not agree to do so, James Madison was elected president.

At the end of his second administration, Jefferson was depressed. His dream of gaining commercial rights for America by peaceful means had vanished. During his presidency, towns, cities, and industries had grown at a quickened pace. He thought about America's farming communities and wrote later, "Experience has taught me that manufactures are now as necessary to our independence as to our comfort."

A stack of bills lay on his desk to read and sign or veto before Congress adjourned. He wrote his friend, French economist P. S. du Pont de Nemours, "Within a few days I retire to my family, my books, and farms and having gained the harbor myself, I shall look on my friends still buffeting the storm, with anxiety indeed, but not with envy. . . . Nature intended me for the tranquil pursuits of science, by rendering them my supreme delight."

On March 4, 1809, James Madison invited Thomas Jefferson to ride with him to the inauguration. Jefferson refused, saying that it was Madison's day as president. But Jefferson did attend the inaugural ball for President Madison and other gala parties where many of his friends said good-bye to him.

Jefferson still had papers and books to pack, besides three wagonloads of shrubs and seeds to send home. When at last he reached Monticello, his family and all the grandchildren were waiting for him.

There was Francis Eppes, son of his deceased daughter Maria; Martha and Thomas Mann Randolph, Jr., and their eight children (Martha eventually had eleven by 1818); Martha Carr, his widowed sister, and her six children; as well as Jefferson's younger sister Anna (Mrs. Hastings Marks). The Marks lived in the area and visited often. Jefferson could finally enjoy them all in his retirement years.

Granddaughter Virginia Randolph Trist wrote later about the fun the children had racing around the terrace and lawn. The youngest and smallest were given a head start, and the winners rewarded with dried fruit — figs, prunes, and dates — three to the victor, two to the second, and one to the lagger who came in last.

Jefferson loved his grandchildren and spent hours playing, teaching, and sharing the secrets of nature with them. The older boys rode horseback alongside him; the younger ones rode on his knee.

His sister Martha and her family stayed at Monticello after 1809, although their home was Edgehill. Martha had faithfully served as both hostess and housekeeper for Jefferson throughout the years, and she continued to greet his many visitors.

Jefferson's mansion was finished now and it was almost three times the size of the original two-story dwelling of eight rooms. He had enlarged the library, and added extra rooms for the children and the constant visitors.

People from all positions in life came to talk to the "Sage of Monticello" and often stayed for weeks. Jefferson would sometimes retreat to his Poplar Forest home, ninety miles away, to escape them.

Not only did they come to talk to this brilliant man, but also to enjoy his home and gardens. Monticello was filled with his creativity. Some of Jefferson's devices were adapted from the inventions of others, such as a weather vane to record the

*The west front of Monticello, painted in the early nineteenth-century.*

wind's direction, "automatic" double glass doors between the entrance hall and parlor, and an unusual seven-day clock above the entrance door that told not only the time but also the day. A folding ladder was used to reach the clock and wind it with a twenty-two-inch wrought iron key.

Jefferson's art collection of paintings and sculptures adorned the hall and parlor. In the tearoom, there were marble busts of Jefferson's heroes — George Washington, John Paul Jones, Benjamin Franklin, and the Marquis de Lafayette. Jefferson's "skyroom," the small eight-sided dome room with a spectacular view, was reached by climbing steep stairs. It was used as a grandson's bedroom.

Of the grandchildren, Martha's oldest son was Jefferson's namesake and favorite. Thomas Jefferson Randolph received the love and affection his grandfather would have lavished on the son he did not have. Jeff was even stronger and taller than Jefferson's father Peter had been. Jefferson personally took him shopping for a new wardrobe and paid the entire cost of his stay in college in Philadelphia, often sending letters of advice.

Jefferson's interest in educating young people had led him to plan a school system for Virginia. He had been named to the board of an academy, organized by Albemarle citizens, for a secondary school near Charlottesville. In 1814, Jefferson drafted plans for the school, which included a design of handsome domed and columned buildings, unusual serpentine brick walls, and a stately rotunda.

At first the Virginia legislature would not consider a charter for a school system, because money was lacking and the country was at war. But by 1817, urged by Jefferson's friends Madison and Monroe, the Virginia legislature passed a bill to incorporate the academy at Charlottesville as Central College. It became the University of Virginia, with Jefferson as its first rector.

Jefferson spent a great part of his time superintending the building construction and rode about three miles from his home to the university

*A view of the University of Virginia; the rotunda Jefferson designed (left) resembles Monticello.*

almost daily. When he wasn't there, he watched the progress of his "academic village" from the northeast corner of the Monticello terrace, through a telescope.

During the bad times of 1819 and 1820 when the banks were failing, Jefferson's loans on his property at the Bank of the United States were called in for payment. Jefferson had also countersigned loans of 20,000 dollars for a friend who went bankrupt, leaving Jefferson with loans that he could not pay.

Jefferson had sold his precious book collection of 7000 volumes to the Library of Congress, after the library was burned by the British during the

War for Independence. His books became the basis of the Library of Congress collection. As Jefferson was now deeply in debt, his grandson Jeff Randolph took over the management of the Albemarle farms.

From time to time Jefferson felt his rheumatism. Yet even in his retirement years, the great man stayed well-informed and influenced political policy. Jefferson wrote volumes of letters to friends, including Madison and Monroe, the two presidents who followed him. Once again he and John Adams corresponded about the nation's problems. He wrote Adams that he had received 1267 letters in a single year. He was also writing his autobiography.

On March 7, 1825, Jefferson's dream was fulfilled when the University of Virginia opened its doors to 123 students. That year, a young New Englander, Joseph Coolidge, came for advice about his career and fell in love with Jefferson's favorite granddaughter, Ellen. It wasn't long before they were married.

While the couple was on their honeymoon, their luggage and wedding gifts, sent to Boston by packet, were lost when the boat sank. One of the lost items was a beautiful hand-carved desk that Jefferson had given them. To console Ellen, and as a "memorial of affection," Jefferson sent her the original folding writing desk on which he had written the Declaration of Independence.

At this time Jefferson needed to raise money to pay his debts and avoid bankruptcy. There were no buyers for his land because of falling prices for farm crops and additional taxes. He asked the Virginia legislature for permission to hold a lottery to sell his property. He wanted to keep Monticello and the farm, and be able to pay his debts. At first the legislature refused him, then agreed, and a lottery was held. Private subscribers (Jefferson's friends) promised funds, and Jeff Randolph took charge of his affairs. Although it took years, his grandson made good on all of Jefferson's debts.

In 1822, Jefferson had fallen and broken his left arm; after that he could not use it again. Both his

*A ticket from the Jefferson lottery, held in April, 1826.*

right and left wrists gave him trouble and he said that a page of writing was a day's work. Jefferson's senses remained keen and his mind clear but, by the end of the year, his health began to give way. When he was younger, he had written, "All my wishes end, where I hope my days will end, at Monticello."

On March 16, 1826, four weeks before he was eighty-three, Jefferson drafted and signed his will. In it he left Francis Eppes land at Poplar Forest and the residue was to be put in trust for Martha, so her husband could not touch it. Martha's brilliant husband, Thomas Mann Randolph, had become mentally unstable. The will also freed five slaves who were skilled workers, and whom Jefferson felt could take care of themselves.

In Boston, John Adams was not well either and Jefferson's last letter to him introduced Jeff, who wanted to meet his grandfather's famous friend. One month before he died, Jefferson wrote his last letter to Madison, committing the special care of the university to him, and said, "To myself you have been a pillar of support thro' life."

By now he could not walk, but three weeks before he died, he went for a hard ride in the woods. Later when Jefferson lay dying on his alcove bed, he told Martha to look in a certain drawer where she would find something intended for her. She found a poem, "A Death Bed Adieu from Th.J. [Thomas Jefferson] to M.R. [Martha Randolph]."

On the evening of July 3, Jefferson hung on to life, asking the doctor, "Is it the Fourth?" and received the reply, "It soon will be." Then an hour before midnight, he asked Nicholas Trist, the husband of granddaughter Virginia, "This is the Fourth?" It was an hour before midnight, but wishing not to disappoint him, Trist nodded assent.

At ten minutes to one on the afternoon of the fourth of July, Thomas Jefferson died. Strangely, John Adams also died that day. It was the fiftieth anniversary of the Declaration of Independence.

*The last portrait of Thomas Jefferson, painted by Thomas Sully.*

*Jefferson's tombstone, in the graveyard at Monticello.*

# Epilogue

"The price of freedom is eternal vigilance."

**W**hether you find Jefferson's image carved on the granite walls at Mount Rushmore in South Dakota, or on the nickel jingling in your pocket, his spirit rings through the ages.

When Jefferson wrote his epitaph, he did not mention the high honors that people had bestowed on him, such as the office of president of the United States. He chose to be remembered for three things he felt were his gifts to the people, and asked that his gravestone read:

HERE WAS BURIED THOMAS JEFFERSON,
AUTHOR OF THE
DECLARATION OF AMERICAN INDEPENDENCE
OF THE
STATUTE OF VIRGINIA FOR RELIGIOUS FREEDOM
AND FATHER OF THE
UNIVERSITY OF VIRGINIA

# Bibliography

*Books for Young People*

Adler, David A. *Thomas Jefferson, Father of Our Democracy*. New York: Holiday House, 1987.

Betts, Edwin M., and James A. Bear, Jr., eds. *Family Letters of Thomas Jefferson*. Columbia, Mo.: University of Missouri Press, 1966, rpt. 1985.

Bober, Natalie. *Thomas Jefferson: Man on a Mountain*. New York: Atheneum, 1988.

Monjo, F. N. *Grand Papa and Ellen Aroon*. New York: Holt, Rinehart and Winston, 1974. Dell Publishing Company, 1990.

Newsweek Books. *Thomas Jefferson: A Biography in His Own Words*, Vols. 1 and 2, *The Founding Fathers*. New York: Newsweek Inc., 1974.

Patterson, Charles. *Thomas Jefferson*. New York: Franklin Watts, 1987.

Beilenson, Nick, ed. *Thomas Jefferson, His Life and Words*. White Plains, NY: Peter Pauper Press Inc., 1986.

Fleming, Thomas J. *The Man from Monticello: An Intimate Life of Thomas Jefferson*. New York: William Morrow and Company, 1969.

Johnson, Samuel. *Johnson's Dictionary*, a Modern Selection. New York: Pantheon Books, 1963.

Malone, Dumas. *Jefferson, The Virginian*, Vol. I, *Jefferson and His Time*. Boston: Little Brown, 1948.

————. *Jefferson and the Rights of Man*. Vol. II, *Jefferson and His Time*. Boston: Little Brown, 1951.

————. *Jefferson and the Ordeal of Liberty*. Vol. III, *Jefferson and His Time*. Boston: Little Brown, 1962.

————. *Jefferson the President, First Term, 1801–1805*. Vol. IV, *Jefferson and His Time*. Boston: Little Brown, 1970.

————. *Jefferson the President, Second Term, 1805–1809*. Vol. V, *Jefferson and His Time*. Boston: Little Brown, 1974.

————. *The Sage of Monticello*. Vol. VI, *Jefferson and His Time*. Boston: Little Brown, 1981.

## Magazines

"Thomas Jefferson." *Cobblestone: The History Magazine for Young People* 10 (1989), no. 9. Peterborough, N.H.: Cobblestone Publishing Inc.

"Independence." *Time* (July 5, 1976), special 1776 issue. New York: Time Inc. Magazines.

## Visual Material

*1776.* Musical on signing of the Declaration of Independence, 141 min., Beta/VHS video. Columbia Pictures, 1972. Distributed by RCA/Columbia Pictures.

## Information Sources
(With special thanks from the author)

*The Huntington Library.* British and American History Collection. 1151 Oxford Road, San Marino, California 91108.

The Thomas Jefferson Memorial Foundation, Inc. A private nonprofit organization, since 1926, that owns and operates Monticello. Monticello, P.O. Box 316, Charlottesville, Virginia 22902.

Daniel P. Jordan, Executive Director; and Cinder L. Stanton, Executive Director of Research, Monticello Foundation.

Robin H. Gabriel, Director of Education, The Thomas Jefferson Visitors Center. (The Education Department is located two miles west of Monticello.)

# Index

*Page references in italics indicate illustrations*